Polarity Intelligence

ENDORSEMENTS

I am excited for everyone who will read *Polarity Intelligence* and everyone who will have a friend or colleague recommend it or a professor require it. You are about to have a transformative experience that will impact your understanding, thinking, knowing, and, most importantly, your actions. That may sound bold until you read on and learn about 100 percent predictability over time! *Polarity Intelligence* is a gift and guide for anyone wondering how to successfully live or lead during chaos, when encountering obstacles, uncertainties, or division. Enjoy!

Bonnie Wesorick, MSN, RN, DPNAP, FAAN
Author and Founder: CPM Resource Center and Consortium

I am excited about *Polarity Intelligence*. Dr. Tracy Christopherson and Michelle Troseth do a masterful job of creating a basic, easy-to-understand introduction to Polarity Thinking as a necessary discipline for effective leadership. And they have done much more. They identify two additional skill sets that are essential: building healthy relationships and practicing meaningful dialogue. Then, Tracy and Michelle provide clear definitions, great application stories as well as guidelines for developing all three sets of leadership skills. Finally, they provide a way to assess progress with each of these skill sets.

Based on years of application experience combined with solid research, Tracy and Michelle not only articulate why polarity intelligent leadership is important; they lay out a challenging yet doable path to get there.

Barry Johnson
Creator: Polarity Maps® and Principles

In *Polarity Intelligence: The Missing Logic in Leadership*, Dr. Tracy Christopherson and Michelle Troseth outline how leaders can stop the issues that happen over and over again by sharing the principles of having a polarity mindset along with the skills to cultivate healthy relationships in our work environments. This is the leadership logic you've been waiting for during these unprecedented times!

Ann Deaton, PhD
Author: *VUCA Tools for a VUCA World*
Developing Leaders and Teams for Sustainable Results

Polarity Intelligence for leaders could not have been published at a more important time. We are facing a crisis of civility in our nation, and we need leaders who have the skills and mindset to bring us back to our common humanity and build a culture of greater equity. Building leaders with a polarity mindset, creating healthy relationships, and engaging in meaningful dialogue is a powerful combination.

Philomena Mantella, PhD
President: Grand Valley State University

Christopherson and Troseth offer a salient guide to problem-solving and decision-making through the polarity lens. They see the world organically—with contradicting tensions for which there is no right or wrong answer to our most complex issues. For them, paralysis and taking sides are not options but opportunities to reframe and find space for harmonizing movement. Their principles and processes stimulate creativity and optimism at a personal, organizational, and societal level to improve communications, gain strategic and operational perspective, and realize that what lies in the periphery of problem-solving is definitely not peripheral. Highly recommended for change agents at all levels of development.

Michael Bleich, PhD, RN, FNAP, FAAN
Chief Executive Officer: NursDynamics, LLC

Polarity Intelligence: The Missing Logic in Leadership is a must-have for both emerging and established leaders. It introduces both a revolutionary mindset and applicable tools that, together, are profoundly game-changing for any individual or organization.

Diana Hendel, PharmD
Former Hospital CEO, Author, and Speaker

Polarities are everywhere. To understand and leverage them is to find creative ways forward instead of getting stuck again and again. Who has that kind of time to waste? *Polarity Intelligence* offers clear, lively, and immensely practical guidance from Dr. Tracy Christopherson and Michelle Troseth who have been developing and teaching this material for years. Their wisdom is particularly evident in their inclusion of sections on relationships and dialogue, which are underappreciated but essential *hows* of working with polarities.

Anthony Suchman, MD
Founder and Senior Consultant: Relationship Centered Health Care
Author: *Leading Change in Healthcare*

Polarity Intelligence is a game-changer for leaders from all institutions and industries. It will open your eyes to a new way of addressing the challenges you face every day, at home and at work, and the skills to be deeply human in leading others. It is filled with perspectives that invite the convergence of your intellect, empathy, and soul. I am exceedingly proud of Dr. Tracy Christopherson and Michelle Troseth, will be adding *Polarity Intelligence* to my treasured library, and will be sharing it with every leader I know. It's a book for every leader.

Renwick Brutus
Wealth Manager: Woodbury Financial Services

I am so grateful to have *Polarity Intelligence: The Missing Logic in Leadership* available at my fingertips as a reference for this essential leadership competency. I have been greatly impacted by the work of Dr. Tracy Christopherson and Michelle Troseth through the years and have used them at different times to teach and coach my teams as well as facilitate client events for some strategic polarity intelligence. *Polarity Intelligence* you are holding is gold and a resource you will come back to again and again. Thank you, Tracy, and Michelle!

Tracy Tucker
Executive Vice President: AMR Management Services

There are so many things I love about this new leadership book by Dr. Tracy Christopherson and Michelle Troseth. Their ability to describe the *dynamic balance* that needs to be leveraged and managed between two interdependent poles and how the invisible energy actually works between them is critical for all leaders to grasp. No one can agree more than me that "tension is good" if you know how to work with it! The principles and skills of healthy relationships and meaningful dialogue, along with a polarity mindset, are essential for a healthy work culture in all venues of work.

David Emerald
Author: *The Power of TED* (*The Empowerment Dynamic*)
Creator-in-Chief: Center for The Empowerment Dynamic

Polarity Intelligence: The Missing Logic in Leadership is a must-read for any leader seeking to navigate polarities in leadership and drive positive change in their organization. Tracy and Michelle have created a practical approach for identifying, mapping, and leveraging polarities to deliver positive outcomes. It is an invaluable resource for improving leadership skills and driving success.

Bob Lawrence
Vice President Product Development & Service, Skytron LLC

Polarity Intelligence is a transformation tool that helps to engage entire teams to advance an organization. It provides a level of clarity that inspires one to embrace and understand their individual impact on success. This happens one person, one team, and one organization at a time. A truly wonderful book that captures the positive impact of reframing your thinking to achieve greater success at work and home. A spectacular read!

Barbara Wadsworth
Chief Operating Officer: Main Line Health

One of the things that is most frustrating for me as a business executive is doing things the same way because "that is the way it has always been done." Maybe there are small improvements for a time but, normally, it is short-lived. Often, organizations make changes in management that start this spin cycle over and over. It is rare that you will find an exceptional leader that can greatly impact the organization over time. We know in our personal lives that this is the definition of insanity, but for some reason, it is accepted in the world of business. *Polarity Intelligence* by its definition is changing your mindset to see it differently and having the skills to act differently. Most importantly, this is duplicatable throughout the organizations that embrace this way of thinking. What Dr. Tracy Christopherson and Michelle Troseth's groundbreaking work has taught us is that these principles are effective no matter what type of business it is.

Daron Gunst
Regional Vice President: Wrench Group

Once upon a time, either/or could be approached in a civil and respectful way . . . and then it couldn't. With *Polarity Intelligence,* authors Christopherson and Troseth provide a road back to both/and discourse for leadership and so much more to offer up what might just be an antidote to our divisive times.

Mark Goulston, MD
Author: *Just Listen*
Discover the Secret to Getting Through to Absolutely Anyone

I am thrilled that *Polarity Intelligence* has emerged from the impactful work of Dr. Tracy Christopherson and Michelle Troseth for leaders everywhere. I had the great fortunate to become "polarity aware" early in my leadership career, and members of my leadership team have now benefited from applying *Polarity Intelligence* to their professional and personal lives through their work with Tracy and Michelle. The way they have pulled all the components together (polarity mindset, healthy relationships, and meaningful dialogue) is genius, for novice and experienced leaders alike.

Maureen Kahn
President and Chief Executive Officer: Blessing Health System

Dr. Tracy Christopherson
and Michelle Troseth

POLARITY
Intelligence

The Missing Logic in Leadership

NEW YORK

LONDON • NASHVILLE • MELBOURNE • VANCOUVER

Polarity Intelligence

The Missing Logic in Leadership

Published in New York, New York, by Morgan James Publishing. Morgan James is a trademark of Morgan James, LLC. www.MorganJamesPublishing.com

Proudly distributed by Publishers Group West®

Morgan James BOGO™

A **FREE** ebook edition is available for you or a friend with the purchase of this print book.

_____

CLEARLY SIGN YOUR NAME ABOVE

Instructions to claim your free ebook edition:
1. Visit MorganJamesBOGO.com
2. Sign your name CLEARLY in the space above
3. Complete the form and submit a photo of this entire page
4. You or your friend can download the ebook to your preferred device

ISBN 9781636981888 paperback
ISBN 9781636981895 ebook
Library of Congress Control Number: 2023936048

Cover & Interior Design by:
Christopher Kirk
www.GFSstudio.com

Photo by:
Ashley Avila Photography

Morgan James PUBLISHING **Builds** with... **Habitat for Humanity** Peninsula and Greater Williamsburg

Morgan James is a proud partner of Habitat for Humanity Peninsula and Greater Williamsburg. Partners in building since 2006.

Get involved today! Visit: www.morgan-james-publishing.com/giving-back

To leaders everywhere
who are committed to supplementing your problem-solving skills
with new ways of thinking and leading
so you can enhance all aspects
of your personal life, work environment,
and the communities of which you are a part.
We are committed to helping you identify
the missing logic in your leadership toolkit
and being guides on
your quest to develop and master
Polarity Intelligence.

And to Jerry Christopherson and Kevin Moore,
our amazing husbands and the best personal assistants
we could ever ask for in life:
We are forever grateful for your unwavering love,
steadfast support, top-notch culinary skills,
and uncanny ability to make us laugh when we need it most.
We love you both so much.

FOREWORD

I remember vividly the day that I was introduced to polarity thinking. I already had some intuitive sense that two opposites could be true at the same time, but polarity thinking provided me with a new distinction that quite literally changed the way I saw the world. I began to see how much of my thinking and my actions were limited by false dichotomies. And I started to realize the inherent nature of paradox in every aspect of life. Indeed, the very source of life—breath—is one of the most fundamental polarities. I had, of course, been naturally integrating inhaling and exhaling my entire life without even consciously recognizing this basic fact. Same with the quotidian tension of rest and activity and the relational paradox of self and other. Even our very brains are structured as two interdependent hemispheres.

Armed with this new distinction, I began to see polarities everywhere. In my personal life, I could see that my wife and I occupied different poles on the control and freedom polarity in the way we were raising our children. Our parenting transformed the moment we could see the upside of integrating what we had unconsciously assumed to be mutually exclusive styles. In my professional life as a CEO, I had a new tool that could effectively cut through complexity. Our organization could now focus on both the long term and the short term without neglecting or over-preferencing either. I could both empower my team and be directive. In my communication, I could be direct and kind. The power of polarity thinking was and has been a game changer for me.

The world is becoming increasingly complex and uncertain. Our job as leaders is to increase the complexity of our thinking at a rate that equals or exceeds the rate of the increasing complexity of our environment. Polarity thinking is a modern articulation of an ancient wisdom tool that allows us to do just that. In *Polarity Intelligence: The Missing Logic in Leadership*, Tracy and Michelle have given us a gift. This book is a valuable addition to the literature on polarity thinking and goes one step further by providing the unique combination of having a polarity mindset along with healthy relationships and meaningful dialogue. It is a practical guide for how to leverage this powerful distinction in leadership. And it is the battle-tested product of two leaders who have been employing this thinking in arguably the most complex industry there is—healthcare.

It is also written by two individuals who themselves have internalized the wisdom and grace of polarity thinking. I had the pleasure of being taught by Barry Johnson, the father of polarity thinking, who said to our group: "When I can see you, I can love you." The book Tracy and Michelle have written is an integration of the head and the heart. It is full of practical applied wisdom complemented with the grace and love that Barry Johnson was referring to. I am so pleased to recommend this book and am so grateful to Tracy and Michelle for giving us this important gift.

Darren J. Gold
Author: *Master Your Code*
The Art, Wisdom, and Science of Leading an Extraordinary Life

TABLE OF CONTENTS

Foreword xiii

1. Why Another Intelligence? 1
   Defining the Components of Polarity Intelligence 6
   Why Business Leaders Need Polarity Intelligence 7
   A Polarized World beyond the Workplace 9
   The Benefits of Becoming a Polarity Intelligent Leader 10
   How to Read This Book 17
2. Problem-Solving: The Leader's Achilles' Heel 21
   The Difference between a Problem and a Polarity 22
      Problems 22
      Polarities 25
      Identifying Polarities 33
      A Strategy for Recognizing Polarities 35

3. How to Develop a Polarity Mindset. 39

    Principles that Govern How Polarities Work. 40

    Mapping a Personal Polarity 53

    Leveraging a Polarity 56

    How Polarities Show Up. 60

4. Healthy Relationships: At the Heart of Polarity Intelligence. 65

    Healthy Relationships Are Transformational 67

    Healthy Relationships Impact Culture and Economy 69

    Principles of Healthy Relationships. 71

5. Gaining Insight and Understanding Through

          Meaningful Dialogue. 91

    Why Meaningful Dialogue? 92

    What is Meaningful Dialogue? 93

    Principles of Meaningful Dialogue 95

6. The Journey of Becoming Polarity Intelligent. 117

    The Three Components of Polarity Intelligence. 118

    Polarity Mindset and Healthy Relationships without

          Meaningful Dialogue 119

    Meaningful Dialogue and Healthy Relationships without

          a Polarity Mindset 122

    Polarity Mindset and Meaningful Dialogue without

          Healthy Relationships 125

7. Monitoring and Measuring the Leveraging of Polarities 133

    Monitoring the Leveraging of Personal Polarities 134

    The Polarity Assessment™ Instrument 135

    Characteristics of the Polarity Assessment 136

8. The Call for Polarity Intelligence in Leadership 147

    Becoming Unconsciously Competent at Polarity Intelligence 149

    Becoming an Exemplary Leader by Embodying

          Polarity Intelligence 153

    Evolving with a Polarity Intelligent Leadership Community 158

Polarity Intelligent Leaders: The Hope for Our Future 159

About the Authors. 163
Acknowledgments 165
Addendum 169
   Definitions. 169
      Polarities 169
      Polarity Intelligence 169
      Polarity Mindset. 170
      Meaningful Dialogue 170
   Polarity Intelligence Principles 171
   Polarity Map. 173

1

WHY ANOTHER INTELLIGENCE?

*We cannot solve our problems with the same thinking
we used when we created them.*
Albert Einstein

n the early to mid-1990s, the healthcare system was under fire. Society
was calling for healthcare reform due to patient safety, increasing costs,
waste, and accessibility issues. These were chaotic times, and those in
the healthcare industry were experiencing significant amounts of change.

Like many other industries of the time, the healthcare industry
was impacted by a Newtonian worldview. In a Newtonian worldview, a
system is broken down into parts and designed to function predictably.
All elements of such systems are viewed as fixed and stable, capable of
being analyzed and measured.

As a result, the healthcare system was designed and described as locations (hospital, home, clinic, office), and hospitals were composed of units that treated diseases and broken parts (intensive care, cardiology, orthopedics, and oncology, for example). Some of those units treated age groups (say, neonatal and pediatric), and some units addressed time-related needs (inpatient vs. outpatient). Each unit operated independent of the others and addressed different needs.

Most importantly, care delivery was built upon a medical model which focused on the absence of disease. You might argue that being focused on the absence of disease is not a bad thing in the field of medicine. And you'd be right. In fact, this focus resulted in great advances in medicine, including the development of ways to prevent certain diseases and finding treatments and cures for others. Body parts even became replaceable.

But there's absence of disease, and there's health—the harmony of physical, psychological, sociocultural, and spiritual dimensions. The healthcare system of the nineties was neither focused on health, nor was it a healthy work environment for the healthcare workforce.

The way the system was designed led to transactional relationships among team members, and those between leaders and staff were hierarchical or power based, often supported by sprawling org charts that donned office walls—just in case someone had forgotten their place in the system.

That was the world where we (Tracy and Michelle) cut our teeth as emerging leaders.

At the time, we had a mentor named Bonnie Wesorick. She was a nurse with extraordinary vision and a leader who had a profound influence on the culture at our Midwestern hospital. Bonnie's quest to transform the healthcare system soon spread to others in the industry. And her approach to leading transformation provided us with a new lens through which we would look at the world around us.

We had no way of knowing back then how Bonnie's influence would impact our views of life and leadership, and that we would eventually start a company where we would focus our energy on teaching this approach to leaders in various industries.

* * *

Bonnie saw the flaws in the healthcare system. She realized that using a "more of the same... but different" approach, along with quick fixes, wasn't going to create the healthcare system that was needed. We couldn't transform the system without changing our Newtonian thinking and charting a new direction.

So, she set her mind on creating new infrastructures, processes, and tools that would transform both the healthcare system and the work culture within that system. Bonnie realized what was absent in the healthcare system was a quantum worldview. Leaders had to look at the whole picture rather than the parts, recognize the connectedness of the system, and embrace uncertainty, continuous learning, and randomness.

She wasn't alone in seeing this need for change and this new way of thinking. In our organization and in others, there was a growing awareness that the healthcare industry needed an adjustment, a paradigm shift. In other words, our ways of thinking about and approaching the flaws in the system needed to shift.

What we had always done would no longer work.

Leaders and staff needed a culture that allowed us to use quantum thinking and see the issues from all sides. We needed a holistic approach to healthcare, one that would incorporate body, mind, and spirit. We also needed to be clear about our mission, and everything we did would have to center on that mission.

Naturally, these changes would be built upon strong partnering relationships. Bonnie rallied a group of passionate, like-minded leaders to help solve the problems associated with the old paradigm. We were fortunate to be among that group.

At first, the solutions our group implemented resulted in Positive Outcomes (a key element we'll be discussing). Over time, though, we also experienced unintended negative consequences. Once we began seeing this pattern and noticed recurring challenges, we realized that something was missing. Our approach to moving from Newtonian thinking to quantum thinking did not result in the sustainable outcomes we had hoped for.

Our awareness of this shortfall and our understanding of the significance of this realization increased tenfold when we met Barry Johnson, an organizational development expert who had for many years been studying a phenomenon he referred to as Polarity Thinking™.

Barry helped us to recognize that many of the challenges we faced were not problems that could be solved. He explained that some challenges were polarities, and that a polarity represents a pair of interdependent alternatives. Polarity thinking helps you see that you need to leverage both these alternatives to reach the best outcome.

At the time, we didn't know anything about Polarity Thinking. And because we didn't know what we didn't know, we viewed the challenges we were experiencing as problems that needed to be solved. We lacked the awareness that the healthcare system needed both Newtonian and quantum thinking for the outcomes we desired to be sustainable. We employed either/or thinking by suggesting a paradigm shift from Newtonian to quantum thinking was the solution to the challenges we faced.

But seeing the world through the lens of polarities required us to shift from either/or thinking to both/and thinking so we could understand and leverage the interdependent alternatives present in our organization's culture.

None of that first group of leaders Bonnie had assembled realized that we were facing a missing logic in believing our challenges were problems that *always* had a solution, and that this belief limited our ability to achieve sustainable results over time.

You might be in the same boat as we were back then, throwing resources to the wind trying to solve problems that simply cannot be solved for the mere fact that they are, in fact, polarities that you will need to leverage. Instead of a shifting paradigm, it's essential to embrace both/and thinking to understand and leverage the polarities present in the culture.

This radical shift in seeing the world is the focus of this book.

* * *

Over the years of working with leaders across North America, we've realized that understanding and knowing polarities—including how to leverage them—is far from enough. Using a polarity mindset requires that you engage other stakeholders in meaningful dialogue about your differing points of view. And engaging in meaningful dialogue requires having healthy relationships that foster a shared commitment to a Greater Purpose (another key element we'll be diving into later).

These insights led us to the conclusion that the missing logic in leadership is not just learning to think in terms of polarities and to look at challenges through a polarity lens. What leaders require is to develop Polarity Intelligence.™[1]

In 2018, almost thirty years after we first started having conversations with Bonnie Wesorick and others about how to improve the well-being of our workplaces, we founded MissingLogic® to promote the wisdom of applying Polarity Intelligence to create healthy and healing work cultures.

---

1   Christopherson, T. & Troseth, M., (Hosts). *Healthcare's MissingLogic* [Audio Podcast] Episode 106: Is Problem-Solving the Most Valuable Skill a Leader Can Have? (July 21, 2021)

While the focus of our work started out in the healthcare industry, Polarity Intelligence can be applied to all industries and even to day-to-day living. And while we will explain these concepts in depth in the chapters that follow, knowing what each of the components represents would be helpful.

Defining the Components of Polarity Intelligence

Polarities

Polarities are interdependent pairs of values, perspectives, or points of view that appear contradictory but need each other over time to achieve a Greater Purpose that neither could achieve alone. These seemingly contradictory viewpoints can also be referred to as Poles.

Polarity Intelligence

Polarity Intelligence is an intuitive ability to recognize polarities and to understand and balance through healthy relationships and meaningful dialogue the invisible energy between two Poles. This requires that you transcend personal biases in order to achieve a Greater Purpose.

Polarity Mindset

Recognizing not all challenges are problems to be solved—some are polarities to leverage. The ability to differentiate between a problem and a polarity while understanding and applying the principles that govern polarities so you can attain a dynamic balance and achieve a Greater Purpose.

Healthy Relationships

Relationships that are intentional and centered on a shared purpose. Healthy relationships recognize the human capacity in each other and that we are all equally responsible to achieve a shared purpose. Such relationships honor the need to create balance between being in relationship with yourself and with others and to create trust by being trustworthy. Healthy relationships are soul-connected and bring out the best in one another.

Meaningful Dialogue

Dialogue is a conversation between two or more people where the parties listen and share in a way that leads to deep understanding and shared meaning. Meaningful dialogue begins with setting intentions and creating an environment for psychological safety and exploration. Meaningful dialogue requires listening and awareness, advocacy and inquiry, candor and diplomacy, as well as silence and reflection.

Why Business Leaders Need Polarity Intelligence

At the time we are writing this book, we are three years into the COVID-19 pandemic. The world no longer has a sense of normal, and you may not feel a sense of normality for quite some time to come. Instead, you are living in a volatile, uncertain, complex, and ambiguous (VUCA) world.

The acronym was first used in the military, but it is now widely used in the business world. Each element of the acronym has unique features and causes, and each element requires unique approaches to mitigate its impact.[2, 3] It represents the types of challenges, conditions, and situations that we all face, whether as individuals, teams, leaders, managers, or organizations.

As you read the descriptions below, consider a leadership challenge you are facing and whether it fits these descriptions.

---

2   Bennett, N. & Lemoine, G.J. "What VUCA Really Means for You." *Harvard Business Review.* January–February 2014

3   Bennett, N. & Lemoine, G. J. 2014, "Managing in a VUCA World." From MindTools.com

Table 1. VUCA

Volatile	A challenge or change that is fast-paced, unexpected, unpredictable, and that has an unknown duration
Uncertain	The ability to anticipate, plan, and make predictions about the future is diminished because what is known is becoming irrelevant
Complex	Situations and challenges are multilayered with many interconnections and dependencies, making it difficult to uncover the complete picture and identify a clear path
Ambiguous	There is a lack of clarity. The abundance of unknowns and gray areas represented in contradictions and paradoxes make decision-making challenging

Even if the challenge you are facing fits just a couple of these descriptions, the fact that it has not yet been solved may mean that it will require you to think in new ways. Living in a VUCA world calls for new ways of operating.

Many of the challenges you face simply cannot be solved using just either/or thinking and problem-solving skills. Instead, they require both/and thinking. They require that you are polarity intelligent.

This challenge and others you face will be ongoing. They will have interdependencies that require both/and thinking. And these interdependencies must be leveraged and managed over time.

Without identifying the interdependencies inherent in these situations, you may have an accurate picture of the situation, yet it is incomplete. Having an incomplete understanding of the issues before you can result in false choices. It can lead to unsustainable outcomes and unintended consequences—just like our team faced in the nineties.

But like Bonnie Wesorick's original team that was trying to solve problems that simply cannot be solved, simply understanding and knowing polarities is also not enough. We now know having healthy relationships and meaningful dialogue are also crucial components in this quest for a better world.

Building healthy relationships and being intentional about meaningful dialogue within your workforce and with others in your community fosters a commitment to a shared purpose. It helps you to be more open to diverse perspectives and experiences—an essential skill when managing a winning team. It is equally important for maintaining a thriving work culture, overcoming biases, and combating the overwhelm and anxiety brought on by VUCA conditions.

A Polarized World beyond the Workplace

Being a polarity intelligent leader goes beyond the workplace, though. If you are human, you are experiencing polarized views in your family, community, and nation due to differences in values and points of view.

If you have become fearful of the unknown and of the potential loss of what is familiar to you and what you highly value, it may be that the volatility, uncertainty, complexity, and ambiguity at this time in history are contributing to the distress you experience when faced with differing values or polarized points of view.

The issues that have been dominating the news the past few years in the United States and beyond—the pandemic, political tensions, increasing violence, mass shootings, even the #MeToo and Black Lives Matter movements—have amplified the tension between individuals with differing perspectives, even among families and within marriages.

No matter your political views, if you only view these differences as problems to be solved, these issues will lead to debates that perpetuate either/or thinking and confirmation bias. You may have experienced this firsthand over the past few years. Everyone seems to simply be digging their heals in deeper on their side of the either/or spectrum.

How do you move forward in a healthy way? You approach the issues with a polarity mindset. And to strengthen your relationships, you engage in meaningful dialogue. As a leader, this provides you with the skills to cultivate a culture that recognizes the tension for what it is, understands the energy that binds two interdependent perspectives, and takes steps to leverage the tensions inherent in polarities.

Taking this path allows you to achieve a Greater Purpose.

* * *

Whether at home, in your community, or at work, when you as a leader develop Polarity Intelligence, you naturally foster a culture founded in healthy relationships and supported by meaningful dialogue. In such a culture, individuals will be open to considering other perspectives. They will welcome learning so they can understand differing points of view.

There are also other distinct benefits to growing in Polarity Intelligence.

The Benefits of Becoming a Polarity Intelligent Leader

Polarity Intelligence Reveals Values and Biases

Developing Polarity Intelligence connects you to your personal and deeply held values. It forces you to examine how you developed those values and why they are so important to you. It also calls for you to examine the beliefs that are influencing your preferences.

By being aware of and understanding your values, beliefs, and biases, you can see the possibility of stepping outside of the box that informs your point of view. Doing so allows you to see what you may have never seen before.

Polarity Intelligence Provides a Common Language

The world is full of polarity thinkers—individuals who think *both/and* rather than *either/or*. Polarity thinkers are naturally aware of the interdependencies between values. Not only do they see those interdependencies; they intuitively understand that both Poles are equally important. They may even go so far as to take the actions needed to achieve the best outcomes associated with each value.

In teaching on Polarity Intelligence for decades, we've found that many people do feel the tension between two values but are unaware that they are experiencing a polarity. They may have even tried to relieve the tension between such values. Believing they are dealing with a problem that they must solve, they end up failing and experiencing the same issues over and over.

Without exception, whenever we speak at conferences about polarities, someone in the audience will say, "You've finally put into words what I've been experiencing," or "Now I know how to describe what I've been experiencing." We also often hear, "I've always known it is important for leaders to hold opposing perspectives simultaneously, but until now, I've never had a name for it."

"I've always known it is important for leaders to hold opposing perspectives simultaneously, but until now, I've never had a name for it."

Because all polarities share the same principles and act in the same way, it is possible to clearly articulate not only what the components of a polarity are but also what it feels like to experience a polarity.

This provides a common language and consistent terms for you to describe what you are experiencing, both individually and collectively. It also helps you to determine the meaning of what you are facing.

Polarity Intelligence Makes the Invisible Visible

Barry Johnson—the organizational development expert whom we referred to earlier—developed the initial principles and mapping process for polarities. He created the Polarity Map® (see Figure 1) that represents all aspects of a polarity, including how the polarity works.

Barry believed that if you could *see* the polarity, you could *understand* it, and understanding a polarity would allow you to learn to *leverage* it.

Being able to leverage a polarity to its best advantage allows you to achieve your desired outcome and attain a Greater Purpose. Best of all, it also allows you to sustain the outcomes.

A Polarity Map is an instrument used to define and describe the interdependent pair of values in a polarity, along with the outcomes associated with those values. It provides an early warning system and helps you see strategic steps that can be used to leverage the tension between the two values. We describe this important process in Chapter 2.

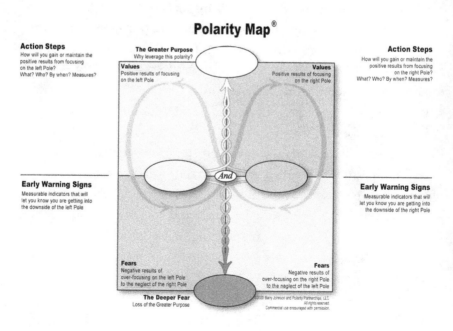

Polarity Map®

Figure 1: A Polarity Map

Barry often refers to the Polarity Map as a wisdom organizer. When you are exploring polarities, the map captures the perspectives of the stakeholders. It shows how the interdependent relationship between the Poles work. The map also provides a visual representation and common language to help stakeholders understand their experiences. We provide a detailed description of the components of the map in Chapter 2, and in Chapter 3, we explain how to use the map to understand how polarities work.

The Polarity Map can also serve as the foundation for a Polarity Assessment™, which we'll discuss in Chapter 7. When you make a polarity visual, you can then better explore and evaluate how well an individual or a team is managing that polarity.

The assessment helps you to clearly see where the tension between the pair of values sits and how frequently the outcomes associated with each value are being experienced. This makes the experience of a polarity concrete. It also makes visible that which you are experiencing, albeit as an individual, family, a department, a leadership team, or as an organization.

Polarity Intelligence Allows You to Move Beyond the Obvious

Your experiences with others shape your beliefs and your values. In turn, those beliefs and values shape your worldview as well as how you interpret the new situations and challenges you experience.

When you feel threatened by opposing points of view, your brain tries to protect you by looking for information that aligns with what you believe and value. It does so to validate what you believe to be true, to confirm what you trust.

Polarity Intelligence enables you to see connections between perspectives that may appear contradictory, connections that aren't obvious to those who aren't polarity thinkers. What's more, Polarity Intelligence allows you to move beyond the obvious. It enables you to access deeper levels of wisdom that come from considering contradictory perspectives.

This movement beyond the obvious allows you to see a more complete picture of your current reality rather than to cling to the belief that your limited point of view is right or complete.

Polarity Intelligence Leverages Conflict, Welcomes Diversity, and Honors Differences

Being polarity intelligent teaches you that you can leverage the tension between conflicting points of view and achieve a Greater Purpose— something you cannot achieve without considering *both* points of view.

When you first notice two points of view and see this as a problem, it leads you to experience tension within. And when you assume this tension is negative, you naturally want to avoid entertaining these differing viewpoints.

But when you see this tension as a potential lever for generating new insights, you embrace these ideas instead. Doing so allows you the chance not only to draw on these fresh insights but also to achieve a shared purpose with someone who holds an opposing view.

Once this happens, you no longer try to resolve the tension. Instead, you welcome and embrace the differing perspectives and leverage the tension.

Individually, each point of view can be correct; however, without the opposing perspective, you are left with an incomplete picture of reality. On the other hand, when you invite diverse points of view, it helps you generate a complete picture of reality.

It is not enough to simply leverage, welcome, and honor differences, though. Being polarity intelligent requires a commitment to a shared purpose. It also requires that you intentionally engage in meaningful dialogue and healthy relationships. Doing so allows you and those in your sphere of influence to agree on a shared purpose so you can achieve what you cannot achieve independently.

Polarity Intelligence Transmutes Fear into Courage

It's natural to fear losing what you value—that which is represented in your point of view. This is why you hold on so tightly to your perspective on a matter. Deep down, you may actually fear that if others pay more attention to what appears to be contradictory to your deeply held values, you may lose not only *what* you value but that you may even lose *your* value.

Some individuals in power positions have mastered the act of manipulating fears to divide and conquer. But when you are polarity intelligent, you realize that both perspectives are right and necessary, that you need both viewpoints to achieve a Greater Purpose. This allows you to transmute your fears into courage. You can let go of your fears as you realize you don't have to *give up* your point of view; instead, you can add to it.

In the process, your fears are transformed. They become the courage to develop a deeper understanding of the current reality. How? Through meaningful dialogue about the opposing perspectives. This allows you to leverage the tension in service of the Greater Purpose.

Polarity Intelligence Provides Evidence for Hope

Living in a polarizing environment—albeit at work, with family, community, or in your country—can be an isolating experience. Whether this polarization is real or not, you might choose *not* to engage with those you know or assume to have an opposing perspective simply to avoid conflict. This disengagement can lead to feeling hopeless, as neither party is willing to open themselves up to seeing the accuracy of the other's perspective.

Polarity Intelligence helps you to recognize that one point of view is not more accurate or more important than the other. In doing so, it moves you toward others and ends isolation.

By using the three essential components of Polarity Intelligence—a polarity mindset, healthy relationships, and meaningful dialogue—

you not only strengthen relationships at a deeply human level but also enhance a collective connection to a Greater Purpose.

This can only be achieved through the benefits of *both* perspectives, though. Leveraging the benefits of both Poles over time leads to sustainable Positive Outcomes. In turn, this provides evidence for hope.

Polarity Intelligence Predicts Future Outcomes

Wait, what? Once you understand polarity principles, you know that *all polarities work the same way.* It's like the principle of gravity. You know that when you drop something, it *will* fall to the ground. Polarities are similar.

As you grow in Polarity Intelligence, you'll begin to apply the principals even broader. Once you've done the work to determine what the polarity is and you can describe it in detail, you will be able to predict what will occur over time based on the actions you chose to take or *not* take. (Don't worry, this will all become clearer as you work through this book.)

Having the ability to use Polarity Intelligence to predict what will happen is like having a crystal ball that can show you the future. This is precisely what has fueled our passion for equipping leaders with this essential competency. As a polarity intelligent leader, you will be able to see future outcomes, and because you can see those outcomes, you can create strategic plans to get you to those outcomes.

Having this skill builds trust. It also enables you to preempt problems and make changes to avoid unintended negative consequences.

Polarity Intelligence Speeds Up Transformation

Remember Bonnie Wesorick and the challenges our team faced? Once we implemented insights from having a polarity mindset, Bonnie went on to publish multiple papers and a book on polarities in healthcare. She declared, "Polarity Thinking™ in its simplicity is magical."

At its simplest form, the magic of Polarity Intelligence lies in differentiating *problems* from *polarities*. Being able to distinguish between problems and polarities keeps you from trying to address the same challenges over and over.[4]

The complexity within Polarity Intelligence is transformational. Once you have a deep understanding of how polarities work, you will not only be able to leverage Early Warning Signs, make course corrections, and avoid unintended negative consequences, but you will also be able to respond *fast*. As a result, transformation is sped up.

Earlier, we had mentioned a Polarity Assessment that we'll discuss in Chapter 7. In that chapter, we'll show you how the assessment will help make the *experience* of the polarity visible and give you *real-time diagnostic information*, both of which enable you to leverage the polarity and respond rapidly.

Whether you use a Polarity Assessment or simply monitor how frequently you are experiencing the Outcomes and Early Warning Signs identified in your Polarity Map, you'll be able to respond faster to leverage the polarities around you. This rapid response speeds up the transformational process precisely because you have a deeper awareness of *what* you or your organization is experiencing and *why*.

Having such a clear picture of your current reality also enables you to do an early and frequent evaluation of Action Steps. This, in turn, reduces unintended negative consequences caused by ineffective strategies.

How to Read This Book

We know learning a new paradigm and all its details can be a lot to take in—but trust us, it will be worth it. That's why each chapter has been written in an intentional order. If this is your first time reading this book, it would help if you to read the chapters in sequential order. Once

---

4   As a reminder, problems can be *solved* but polarities must be *leveraged*.

you've done that, you can always go back and concentrate on the chapters that help you to develop your Polarity Intelligence. You'll also find a few reflection questions and action steps at the end of each chapter to help you process and apply what you're learning.

Chapter 2 focuses on helping you to **develop a polarity mindset**. Having a polarity mindset will allow you to differentiate between a problem and a polarity. It will also help you identify polarities in all areas of your life.

Once that you can identify polarities, **Chapter 3** describes the principles of **how polarities work**.

We've established that being polarity intelligent is not only about having a polarity mindset, it also requires working closely with others. Being skilled at developing healthy relationships plays a key role in your growth as a leader equipped with Polarity Intelligence. Hence, **Chapter 4** introduces you to the **principles of healthy relationships**. It also establishes why such relationships are an important component of being polarity intelligent.

At the heart of healthy relationships lies meaningful dialogue. **Chapter 5** introduces you to **how meaningful dialogue enables you to uncover and explore polarities**, a skill fundamental to Polarity Intelligence.

Next, **Chapter 6** provides the rationale for **why a polarity mindset, healthy relationships, and meaningful dialogue are essential elements of Polarity Intelligence**.

Chapter 7 increases your awareness of the importance of measuring the present-day experience of the polarities for all stakeholders. Being able to do so allows you to **do a real-time assessment of the effectiveness of your action strategies**.

Finally, **Chapter 8** describes how to know when you are in the presence of a **polarity intelligent leader**.

* * *

At the start of this chapter, we mentioned what a difference it made as emerging leaders at a hospital in the Midwest region of the United States when we realized that the challenges we were facing weren't problems we could solve; they were polarities we had to leverage.

Being able to see the difference between a problem and a polarity is the first step in your journey to becoming a polarity intelligent leader. That is what we turn to next.

2

PROBLEM-SOLVING:
THE LEADER'S ACHILLES' HEEL

The notion that all of these fragments are separately existent
is evidently an illusion, and this illusion cannot do anything
other than lead to endless conflict and confusion.
David Bohm | *Wholeness and the Implicate Order*

To develop Polarity Intelligence, you must be able to recognize polarities. Before you can recognize a polarity, though, you must know what it is. You must also know how it is different from a problem.

Whether you know it or not, you've been solving problems since the day you were born. When you were hungry or uncomfortable, you cried.

Then someone showed up and solved the problem for you. They either fed you or they comforted you.

You learned to solve problems for yourself as you matured. And as you grew in your leadership skills—even as a child—you learned to solve problems for others as well.

Problems are easy to spot and solve for most leaders. But if you misdiagnose a *polarity* as a problem, you can be left trying to solve the same issue over and over, never finding a sustainable solution. This can cost you time, money, and energy.

Misdiagnose a polarity as a problem and you can be left trying to solve the same issue over and over, never finding a sustainable solution.

In this chapter, we'll not only explain the differences between a problem and a polarity, we will also give you a process for differentiating between the two. We will break down the anatomy of a polarity and use a Polarity Map to apply it to a real-life polarity. By the time you finish this chapter, you will have the tools you need to recognize a polarity.

The Difference between a Problem and a Polarity

Problems

In 2018, Michelle and I (Tracy) left our corporate jobs in the healthcare industry and started MissingLogic. Combined, we had close to sixty years of coaching and consulting experience working with healthcare organizations across North America. We were excited to leverage our knowledge and experience to help leaders manage the challenges they routinely faced in healthcare.

Like many startups, ours was a small operation. Not only were we the founders, we were also the only employees. When we were not being efficient in our execution of tasks, it led to us being swamped, which led to hiccups in workflow, which, in turn, resulted in delays in deliverables. This bottleneck was getting in the way of our business growing.

This was a problem we needed to solve. If we were to grow and scale our business, we had to find a way to reduce dependency on us as the founders.

Perhaps you can relate.

As a leader, you face problems every day and you solve them. That is what you do—leaders solve problems. Your ability to problem solve is what sets you apart. It is your superpower. This superpower also includes your ability to help your team solve problems. You might even be able to draw a direct comparison between your ability to solve problems and your success as a leader.

Though you solve them all the time, do you know what constitutes a problem?

The Anatomy of a Problem

A problem is a challenge. It can be something unpleasant that you want to avoid, change, or solve because you feel it is interfering with achieving the outcomes you desire. Problems are solvable; they have an endpoint. And to find that endpoint, you must find the right solution.

As for the approaches you have for solving a problem, they are independent of each other—they can stand on their own; they do not need to be coupled with any of the other approaches.

Here's an easy example using the problem of being hungry during my workday. To satiate my hunger, I can find something to eat at home. Or I can head to Panera Bread, a favorite go-to lunch spot of mine. I can also use a meal-delivery app and have lunch brought to me.

To solve my problem, I must pick *one approach* out of the three. These options are independent of each other. I either eat what I have at home, go out to have lunch, or have it delivered. Once I've picked the approach that works for me on a particular day, my problem is solved.

Solving problems require either/or thinking. Either one approach will work or another will. While you might have multiple approaches to choose from, you choose the option you believe is going to give you the outcome you desire. You implement what you discern to be the best solution. If at first that solution doesn't work, you try another until your problem is solved.

When it came to solving the problem of the bottleneck in our business, Michelle and I had several alternatives. The most cost-efficient option was to hire a contractor or two to take care of administrative tasks. This would free up time for us to focus on tasks that only we could do. A more costly option was to hire an entrepreneurial individual or two who would add value, bringing knowledge and experience that would supplement—even supersede—what we had. We chose to go with the first option. This solved the bottleneck and allowed our company to grow.

So how does this relate to the problems you might face and solve every day?

As a leader, you have had a lot of practice at identifying and solving problems. We already talked about others solving your problems for you when you cried as a baby. As a toddler, you began to have problems presented to you in the form of questions: "Where's your nose? Your eyes? Your ears?" Soon, these progressed to questions such as, "What color is this?" You quickly learned that solving the problem meant providing the correct answer.

Once in school, you continued to be taught to solve problems—presented as tests and assignments—by providing the correct answer. When you gave the right answer, you were rewarded.

All along, you came to believe that every problem has only *one* correct answer, a singular solution. Anything but that correct answer is the *wrong* answer. In your mind, solving a problem meant finding the correct answer to a question.

Over time, you learned

- if your answer is right, the opposite answer is wrong,
- any challenge you face is a problem to be solved,

- that it is very important to solve problems,
- when you solve problems, you will be rewarded.

As a result, whenever a challenge arises—personally, in your family, home, community, organization, and your country—your first response is to see the challenge as a problem. And once you see a problem, you automatically look for the right answer or singular solution.

That is where the trouble starts. This is your Achilles' heel: **As a result of the success you've had finding the right answers to problems, you've become confident in your ability to identify problems and solve them.** It's your go-to approach no matter what challenge is before you.

But it's not always that simple. There are times when your solution will not solve the problem, when the problem simply will not go away. The same challenge shows up over and over, sometimes simply in a different disguise.

Not only does the challenge end up being repetitive, it also seems to be unsolvable. Why? Because the problem you are trying to solve is not a problem; it is not solvable. What you are experiencing is a polarity. Problem-solving is a superpower ... until you apply it to a polarity.

Problem-solving is a superpower ... until you apply it to a polarity.

Polarities

So what are polarities? At the core, polarities represent an interdependent pair of values. This concept of interdependence has existed since ancient times. You may be familiar with the Taoist yin and yang symbol, for example. It represents a polarity.

The yin and yang represent the interdependent energies of light and darkness. It acknowledges that what appears to be contradictory can be complimentary. This interrelatedness gives rise to something greater than either element represents on its own.

Figure 2: The yin and yang symbol represents a polarity

Polarities represent an interdependent pair of values that initially appear to be contradictory. The pair is distinctly separate yet bound together by energy in an interdependent relationship; they need each other to achieve a purpose neither could achieve separately.

Polarities are sometimes called paradoxes, dualities, dilemmas, or wicked problems. The interdependent pair of values or perspectives, as you learned in Chapter 1, are often referred to as Poles.

While there are many articles and books on the topic, in our years of coaching and working with leaders, Michelle and I have found that most leaders are unaware of polarities. They are equally uninformed of the impact polarities have on their leadership and the sustainable results they seek.

Dealing with what seems to be unsolvable problems is not only frustrating on an organizational level, but also equally as frustrating on a personal level. The constant pursuit of solutions to impossible problems begins to feel never-ending. Plus, it wastes valuable resources—over and over again. If this is true for you and your team, you are not alone. And rest assured, you don't have to stay in this rut.

Polarity Intelligence can be your new superpower, helping you differentiate between the problems you can solve and the polarities you need to leverage. The first step to developing this superpower is to learn and understand the anatomy of a polarity.

The Anatomy of a Polarity

Problems have a beginning and an end. However, polarities are ongoing; they persist over time. In the interdependent relationship between the Poles, there is no endpoint. You need *both* Poles. Because of that, polarities require both/and thinking.

In Chapter 1, we introduced the Polarity Map. Here, we will use the Polarity Map to explore the anatomy of a polarity. See Figure 2.

You'll notice that we consistently capitalize the components of a Polarity Map, as many of these are trademarked words and phrases.

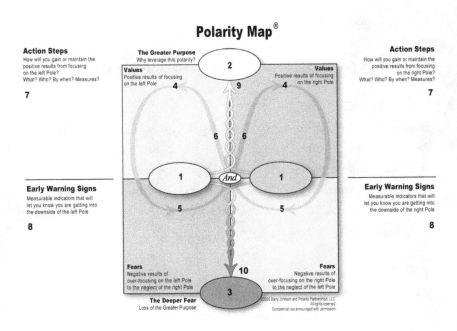

Figure 3: Anatomy of a Polarity

1. The Two Poles

You begin identifying a polarity by defining the two Poles. (You will learn how to do this later in the chapter.) These are an interdependent pair of values. Neither Pole is more important than the other, nor is one positive and the other negative. Because they are both positive, it's important to use neutral terms to represent the Poles.

2. The Greater Purpose

The Greater Purpose is the outcome you ultimately desire to achieve. Doing so is not attainable from either one Pole or the other alone—both Poles must be supported. This represents why it's important to leverage the polarity.

3. The Deeper Fear

The Deeper Fear is the opposite of the Greater Purpose. It represents what's at risk if *both* Poles aren't supported and the polarity isn't leveraged.

4. The Positive Outcomes

There are Positive Outcomes associated with focusing on each Pole. They are the reason we value each Pole and give attention to it. Achieving these Positive Outcomes for both Poles is necessary to achieve the Greater Purpose.

We will sometimes use the term Positive Outcomes and other times the term Upsides through the remainder of this book; they refer to the same key component of a polarity.

5. The Negative Outcomes

When either or both Poles are neglected, you'll experience Negative Outcomes. These also represent what you fear will happen if the Pole you prefer is neglected and attention is given to the other Pole.

We will sometimes refer to the Negative Outcomes as Downsides.[5]

---

5   Again, on the Polarity Map, these are labelled *Fears*, but we prefer using the terms Negative Outcomes and Downsides.

6. The Infinity Loop

The Infinity Loop on a Polarity Map represents the invisible energy that both separates the Poles and binds them together.

7. The Action Steps

The Action Steps represent the actions that must be taken to achieve or maintain the Positive Outcomes of each Pole. In order to leverage a polarity, the Action Steps of both Poles need to be taken simultaneously.

8. The Early Warning Signs

The Early Warning Signs are the alert system that informs you of when you are starting to experience the Negative Outcomes of a Pole. These signs are symptoms of an overemphasis on one Pole to the neglect of the other; they will also show up when the Action Steps have not been effective.

9. The Virtuous Cycle

The intertwined arrows pointing upward toward the Greater Purpose represent the effect of Action Steps supporting the achievement of the Positive Outcomes for both Poles consistently and frequently.

10. The Vicious Cycle

The intertwined arrows pointing downward toward the Deeper Fear represent how neglecting Early Warnings will lead to consistently and frequently experiencing Negative Outcomes.

To solidify how the map can provide a visual representation of a polarity, let's look at the metaphor of inhaling and exhaling. Inhaling and exhaling is an intrinsic polarity your body manages all day, every day. You cannot *either* inhale *or* exhale. You must *both* inhale *and* exhale to sustain life. To see how the components of a polarity work together, follow along with this breathing exercise.

> **Exercise**
>
> Nice and slowly, take a couple of deep breaths. Now take a very, very slow and deep breath in. Keep inhaling until you think you cannot possibly go any further. You should feel some tension here. If not, keep inhaling until you do.
>
> Hold that breath for a second, then exhale very, very slowly until you cannot get any more air out of your lungs. Again, you should feel some tension here. If not, slowly force more air out of your lungs until you feel the tension.
>
> Now, return to normal breathing.

Let's look at the Polarity Map in Figure 4 showing the Inhale and Exhale Poles. Notice how the neutral Poles of inhaling and exhaling are labeled on the horizontal axis of the map, the Greater Purpose of sustaining life is at the top of the map, and the Deeper Fear of death is at the bottom of the map.

Next, when you look at the completed Polarity Map in Figure 5, you'll see how your experience of inhaling and exhaling is reflected on the map. The upper quadrants show the Upside of inhaling (i.e., Increased Oxygen), and the Upside of exhaling (i.e., Decreased Carbon Dioxide). The lower quadrants show the Downside of overemphasizing inhaling (i.e., Increased Carbon Dioxide), along with the Downside of overemphasizing exhaling (i.e., Decreased Oxygen).

The tension between inhaling and exhaling—what you felt when you inhaled or exhaled as far as you possibly could—is represented by the Infinity Loop. Typically, you only feel the tension if you are ill, have a breathing disorder, or are intentionally manipulating the inhaling and exhaling cycle to achieve an outcome other than sustaining life. But because your body leverages this polarity every day, the energy remains in the upper quadrants, indicating that you're achieving the Upsides of both inhaling and exhaling. This leads to achieving the Greater Purpose of sustaining life.

Polarity Map®

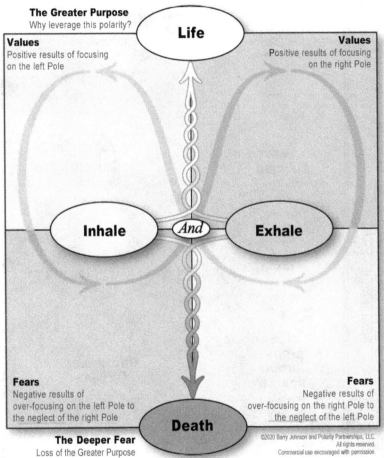

Figure 4: The Inhale and Exhale Poless

Polarities are all around you. They exist in all aspects of your life and in every environment—home, work, community, and country. They are also ongoing. Just like gravity, the energy between the Poles exerts its force on you all the time, whether you are aware of it or not. Polarities are not solvable like problems are. Instead, you need to leverage the energy between the pair to achieve your desired purpose or outcome.

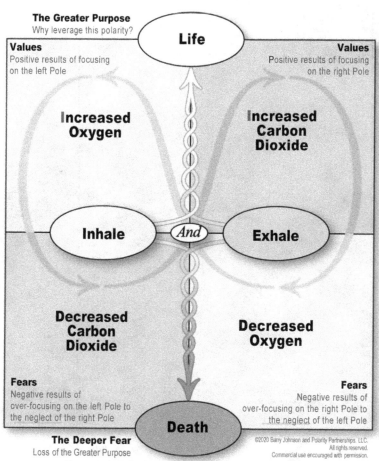

Figure 5: Inhaling and Exhaling Polarity Map

As a leader, you face polarities in every facet of life: your personal life and leadership, your organization, and even in your community and nation. Here are a few examples.

Table 2. Examples of Polarities

Personal Polarities	Leadership Polarities
• Work (Professional Life) and Home (Personal Life) • Activity and Rest • Caring for Self and Caring for Others • Individual and Team • Advocacy and Inquiry	• Directive Decision-Making and Participative Decision-Making • Candor and Diplomacy • Vertical Relationships (Hierarchy) and Horizontal Relationships (Partnership) • Productivity and Relationships • Centralized Processes and Decentralized Processes
Organizational Polarities	**Community/National Polarities**
• Recruitment and Retention • Patient Safety and Staff Safety • Customer Experience and Employee Experience • Process and Progress • Margin and Mission	• Individual Freedom and Common Good • Local and Global • Claiming Power and Sharing Power • Transparency and Security

Identifying Polarities

One of the ways in which problem-solving becomes the Achilles' heel for leaders is the tendency to look at *all* the challenges you face as problems. When you approach challenges with this lens, you only see half of the picture. You make either/or choices, and you use problem-solving skills to try and fix them.

However, a polarity lens requires approaching challenges through a both/and lens so you can see *both* perspectives as well as to notice the interdependence between the Poles. Doing so provides you with a complete picture and allows you to leverage the energy between both Poles.

Let's look at Figure 6 to help us understand why looking through a polarity lens is so essential to developing Polarity Intelligence.

Figure 6: Rubin's Vase Illusion

You may have seen this illustration before. It was developed in 1915 by the Danish psychologist Edgar Rubin. When you look at the picture, do you see two faces? Or do you see a vase?

Both images exist within the illusion. (If you struggle to see *both*, try looking at only the white section or only the black sections and then let your eyes get slightly out of focus.)

If you see the vase, you are accurate. If you see the faces, you are accurate. Both perspectives are accurate yet incomplete. If you do *not* see both perspectives, you have an incomplete picture.

The faces and the vase represent an interdependent pair. If you remove the faces, you are left with a white box. If you remove the vase, you are left with a black box. As a result, you cannot see the faces without the presence of the vase, and you cannot see the vase without the presence of the faces. The two work together to create a whole picture.

The same is true for the Poles represented in a polarity. When you use an either/or problem-solving lens to look at challenges, you may be missing the other half of the interdependent pair. Doing so leads you to base your decisions on an incomplete picture. However, when you use a both/and polarity lens, you are open to the possibility that there is another interdependent perspective, and this allows you to see all aspects of the challenge.

When the challenges you are facing include polarities and you view those challenges only as problems, you are presented with incomplete choices. Over time, this can result in you failing as a leader. It can also lead to the downfall of your team and organization.

When you use an either/or problem-solving lens to look at challenges, you may be missing the other half of the interdependent pair. Doing so leads you to base your decisions on an incomplete picture.

When you use a both/and polarity lens, you are open to the possibility that there is another interdependent perspective, and this allows you to see all aspects of the challenge.

A Strategy for Recognizing Polarities

The next step in developing Polarity Intelligence is to be able to recognize a polarity when you experience it. It takes practice, but you can develop this skill in no time if, when facing a challenge, you ask, "Is this a problem to solve or a polarity to leverage?"

This strategy relates back to the anatomy of a problem and that of a polarity. When faced with a challenge, you can consider these key questions:

1. **Is this an *ongoing* challenge?** In other words, have you or the team faced this before? If the answer is no, your challenge likely is a problem.

2. **Are the approaches you are considering interdependent?** In other words, is there a contradictory perspective that you *must* consider and incorporate? Being open to this possibility gives you the opportunity to not only have an accurate but also a complete perspective. If the answer is no, your challenge likely is a problem.

3. **To achieve a Greater Purpose, do you need the Positive Outcomes of *both* approaches *at the same time*?** If the answer is no, your challenge likely is a problem.

4. **If you focus your attention on *one* of the approaches and neglect the other, will there be a Downside or any Negative Outcomes?** If the answer is no, the approaches are independent, and your challenge likely is a problem.

One way to understand polarities and the power of these questions is to use the metaphor of the Inhale and Exhale Polarity.

1. **Is inhaling and exhaling an ongoing challenge?** Yes, you must do both, all day and all night. There is no endpoint. So inhaling and exhaling is a polarity.

2. **Are inhaling and exhaling interdependent?** Can you choose to just do one or the other? No, they are interdependent. So inhaling and exhaling is a polarity.

3. **To reach a Greater Purpose, do you need the Positive Outcomes of both inhaling *and* exhaling?** Yes, you must inhale to get oxygen into your body, and you must exhale to remove carbon dioxide. To achieve the Greater Purpose of sustaining life, you need the positive benefits of both. So inhaling and exhaling is a polarity.

4. **If you focus on one and neglect the other, will there be negative consequences?** Yes, if you only inhale, you will die, and if you only exhale, you will die. You must have the benefits of both. So inhaling and exhaling is a polarity.

When you experience tension, pause to ask yourself, "Could what I am facing be a polarity?" If it's not clear right away, ask yourself the four key questions.

If you misdiagnose a polarity as a problem, problem-solving will be your Achilles' heel as a leader. It will cause you to use the wrong logic to address the issue—a logic that will not lead you to sustainable results but instead to false choices, which is why being able to distinguish between a problem and a polarity is the first step in developing Polarity Intelligence.

Now that you know the anatomy of a polarity, the next step is to deepen your understanding of how polarities work and how they show up in consistent ways in your environments. We will discuss this in detail in Chapter 3.

Overview

- Problem-solving is an essential leadership skill and a superpower. It is important to apply that skill to solve challenges that have an endpoint.

- When you try to apply your superpower to a polarity, however, problem-solving becomes your Achilles' heel. It can lead to your downfall and even to that of your team and your organization.

- There are countless polarities in your professional and personal life, in your communities, and in your country.

- Differentiating between a problem and polarity is the first step to developing Polarity Intelligence. It is as easy as asking these questions:

  - Is this an ongoing challenge?

  - Are the approaches you are considering interdependent, like inhaling and exhaling? In other words, is there a contradictory perspective that you *must* consider and incorporate?

  - To achieve a Greater Purpose, do you need the Positive Outcomes of both approaches at the same time?

  - If you focus your attention on *one* of the approaches and neglect the other, will there be a Downside or negative unintended consequences?

Reflection Questions

1. Where in your life are you experiencing tension or conflict?
2. What ongoing problems have you been trying to solve? Could those be polarities?

Call to Action

- Name some polarities in your professional and personal life.

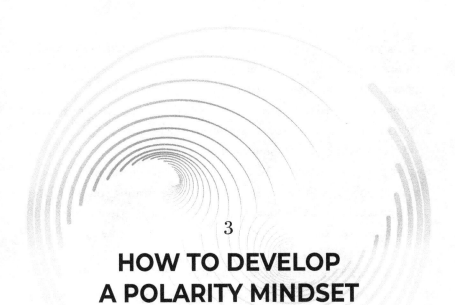

3

HOW TO DEVELOP
A POLARITY MINDSET

*The test of a first-rate intelligence is the ability to hold two opposed ideas
in the mind at the same time, and still retain the ability to function.*
F. Scott Fitzgerald | *The Crack-Up*

I n Chapter 2, you learned what polarities are and how to differentiate polarities from problems. Next to being able to identify a polarity, the most important thing to know as you develop a polarity mindset is that all polarities work the same way. Because they all work the same way, polarities are 100 percent predictable.

We already explained that polarities are like gravity—they are all around you and are acting on you constantly, yet they are invisible. And just like you know that gravity is there because you experience it holding your feet to the ground, the same is true with polarities. You can feel and experience the tension that exists between the Poles.

You also learned how the anatomy of a polarity can be represented in a Polarity Map and how such a map makes the polarity visible.

Next, we are going to show you how you can use a mapping process to see how polarities work. You'll discover the universal principles that govern all polarities. We'll also walk you through creating your first Polarity Map. These are all components of developing a polarity mindset—the first of three crucial components of becoming polarity intelligent.

Principles that Govern How Polarities Work

There are eight universal principles at work in every polarity. To understand these principals and the dynamics of how polarities work—how the Poles interrelate—and to help you experience the shift in energy between the Poles, let's again turn to the metaphor of inhaling and exhaling. Then we will explore a practical example from a challenge we worked on in the healthcare world. Based upon these examples, we will conclude with each of the eight principals.

Let's look again at the Inhale and Exhale Polarity Map (Figure 5).

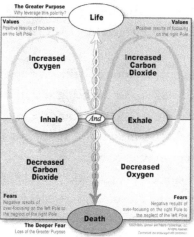

Figure 5: Inhaling and Exhaling Polarity Map

The Greater Purpose of inhaling and exhaling is to sustain life. When you inhale, the Positive Outcome is that your body receives oxygen (top left quadrant). The oxygen then travels from your lungs into your blood.

As your cells use the oxygen to make energy, they also make a gas called carbon dioxide. When you exhale, the Positive Outcome is that you decrease the levels of carbon dioxide in your body (top right quadrant).

You can see this exchange in the map as you follow the Infinity Loop.

As you keep exhaling, though, your body senses a decrease in oxygen (bottom right quadrant), hence you inhale again, looping back to the top left quadrant, and you experience the Upside of inhaling.

The same is true when you keep inhaling. Your body senses the increase in carbon dioxide (bottom left quadrant), hence you exhale, looping back to the top right quadrant to experience the Upside of exhaling.

This is an ongoing cycle. Not only are inhaling and exhaling interdependent; they are also equally important and necessary for you to achieve the Greater Purpose of sustaining life.

Principle 1: Both Poles in a polarity are equally important.

When your body maximizes the Upsides of consistently inhaling *and* exhaling, it leverages the tension between the two Poles. This results in a Virtuous Cycle (seen in the intertwined arrows pointing up between the Poles), which in turn, leads to the Greater Purpose—in this case, sustaining life. Neither Pole can achieve that Greater Purpose on its own.

Principle 2: Alone, neither Pole can reach the Greater Purpose.

The Infinity Loop represents the invisible energy between the two Poles; it shows where the energy is flowing. You can see in the Inhale and Exhale Polarity Map that as you inhale and exhale normally, the energy (represented by the Infinity Loop) is moving between the Poles in the upper quadrants. It illustrates that you are experiencing the Upsides of both inhaling and exhaling (that is, increased oxygen and decreased carbon dioxide) leading to the Greater Purpose of sustaining life. Inhaling or exhaling *alone* cannot take you there.

Principle 3: When the Positive Outcomes of both Poles are achieved, the energy is positive, and it flows toward the Greater Purpose.

Think back to when we asked you to inhale to the point where you felt tension. Your body experienced the Upside of inhaling (that is, receiving oxygen). But as you kept inhaling, the levels of carbon dioxide also rose.

As the carbon dioxide levels rose, you experienced the Downside of only focusing on one Pole (inhaling) while neglecting the other (exhaling). You felt the tension of your body reminding you to also pay attention to the other Pole, alerting you to exhale so you could experience the Upside of exhaling (that is, decreasing the levels of carbon dioxide in your body).

In the Polarity Map in Figure 7, the bold Infinity Loop illustrates how, when you overfocused on inhaling, the energy between the Poles shifted to the lower left quadrant. This indicates you have experienced the Downside of inhaling—too great an increase in carbon dioxide levels.

Note that the position of the bold Infinity Loop around the exhale Pole in the upper right quadrant in Figure 7 has also shifted downward. This illustrates a loss in the Upside of exhaling (decreased carbon dioxide). Physically, you experienced this as tension in your body, and the Polarity Map makes the experience visible.

The tension shows up again when you overfocus on the other Pole—the exhale. (See Figure 8.) When you exhaled to the point where you could expel no more air, you experienced the Downside of exhaling. This resulted in decreasing oxygen, and your body signaled you—expressed as tension—to inhale so you could increase your levels of oxygen to experience the Upside of inhaling.

Feeling the invisible tension is an alert to focus on the other Pole.

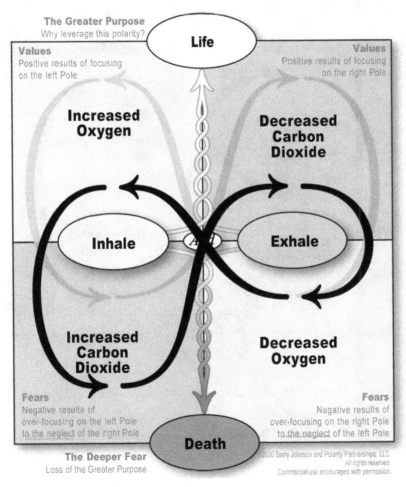

Figure 7: The Downside of Overemphasizing Inhaling

Polarity Map®

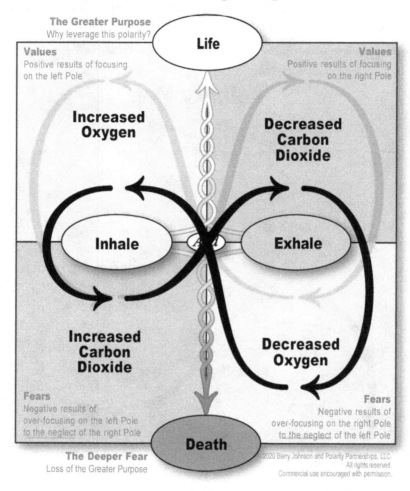

Figure 8: The Downside of Overemphasizing Exhaling

In the Polarity Map in Figure 8, the bold Infinity Loop indicates how overemphasizing your exhale shifted the energy between the Poles to the lower right quadrant, indicating you were experiencing a decrease in oxygen—the Downside of the exhale Pole and loss of the Upside of inhale Pole.

Principle 4: When you overemphasize or overfocus on one Pole and neglect the other, you'll experience the Negative Outcomes of the Pole you focused on.

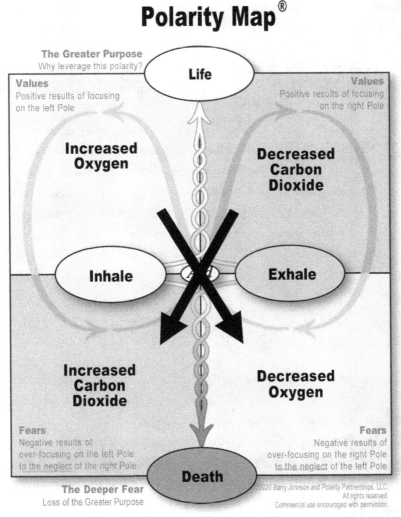

Figure 9: The Loss of the Positive Outcomes

Looking at the map in Figure 9, you can see how overfocusing on either Pole leads to the loss of the Positive Outcomes—shown in the upper quadrants. This is represented in the Negative Outcomes—shown within the lower quadrants of the *opposite* Poles.

Note that the opposite outcomes (e.g., increased oxygen and decreased oxygen) are always placed diagonally to each other in the map. This will be important to remember when you create your own Polarity Maps, as it can help you identify the Negative Outcomes more easily.

Principle 5: The Negative Outcomes of overfocusing on one Pole lead to a loss of the Positive Outcomes of the opposite Pole.

Fortunately, the Inhale and Exhale Polarity is the only polarity where the Deeper Fear is as extreme as it is. *Not* leveraging other polarities won't lead to death. However, the Inhale and Exhale Polarity Map helps you see how significant and powerful the relationship between an interdependent pair of Poles is, and how you must achieve the Positive Outcomes of *both* Poles if you want to reach the Greater Purpose and avoid the Deeper Fear.

The Inhale and Exhale Polarity is also unique in that it is an intrinsic polarity; it is managed automatically. This is not true for other polarities.

* * *

Let's look at an organizational challenge as another polarity example. Early in my career as a leader, I (Tracy) had an experience that will underscore how a Polarity Map can make the invisible visible.

The first project that Michelle and I led together as colleagues was one that involved changing a blood-drawing procedure. The goal was to enable nurses and respiratory therapists in the adult intensive care unit to use their expertise, work collaboratively, and share accountability in caring for patients who had to have their blood drawn.

You may be wondering, *Don't health professionals naturally collaborate?* To some extent, yes. But they often tend to work parallel to each other, each simply carrying out their own tasks. At the time, nurses and respiratory therapists at our hospital didn't necessarily work interdependently.

At one point, Michelle suggested that we engage the nursing and respiratory therapists in the planning process as well as in the decision-making. This level of engagement and shared participatory decision-making was new to me. As a leader, I valued the expediency and autonomy of directive decision-making. So my first reaction was to ask, "Why would we need to involve them? Aren't we the experts?"

Michelle had more experience with shared participatory decision-making. She had experienced its Positive Outcomes, including having access to diverse opinions. She knew first-hand how this could illuminate blind spots, meet staff needs, and increase our understanding of how to leverage the expertise of the staff in the best way possible.

When she shared these possible outcomes with me, I could see the value. What's more, I recognized that the respiratory therapy staff had been complaining that their expertise wasn't being used. They couldn't provide input into decisions, which led to their needs not being considered.

I realized that engaging the nursing and respiratory therapists in the planning and decision-making could also be an answer to a problem the respiratory care department was experiencing.

Thinking I had the solution to our department's problem, I went full speed ahead. The department implemented a shared-governance council to support shared participatory decision-making. I co-led the council. We involved the staff in almost every decision and invested in partnership and dialogue skill development for members of the council. The leadership team even redesigned the department organizational chart.

I felt as if I had been to the top of the mountain and saw what could be on the other side. I wanted everyone else to see it too. I was constantly trying to get others to cross over, to share my perspective.

At first, the department experienced some success. But over time, we began to experience some unintended Negative Outcomes. There was a lack of clarity on the goals—people weren't clear on who was accountable for what. This led to chaos. And sometimes we got stuck in "analysis paralysis," unable to make decisions.

I was so convinced that participatory decision-making was the answer to our problem that I was blind to these unintended consequences. Individuals in the department started to believe this type of decision-making wasn't working. They wanted to shift back to more directive decision-making. Using either/or thinking, I resisted the change. I was afraid we'd lose all the positive benefits we had gained.

What I didn't realize was that the challenge the department faced wasn't a problem that could be solved. I didn't recognize the interdependent relationship between directive decision-making and participative decision-making. And I certainly didn't know that we were dealing with a polarity that required both/and thinking.

If I had known about polarities, if I could have seen our challenge with the help of a Polarity Map, then the interdependent relationships between directive and participative decision-making would have been much clearer.

Figure 10 illustrates this interdependence. It makes visible what I valued about directive decision-making at the start of the project. It also shows what Michelle's experience had led her to value about participatory decision-making. These values—the Upsides—are shown in the upper quadrants. The map also makes clear what the consequences—the Downsides—are when one Pole is overemphasized and the other neglected, as depicted in the lower quadrants.

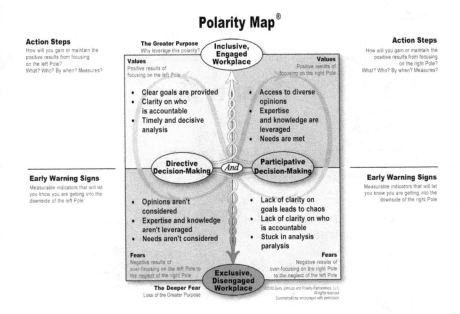

Figure 10: Directive Decision-Making and
Participative Decision-Making Polarity Map

When the respiratory care department overemphasized participative decision-making, we started to experience the Downside (lower right quadrant) of that Pole, which represented the loss of the Upside of directive decision-making (upper left quadrant).

Our team was used to addressing challenges using a problem-solving logic and either/or thinking. This led the team to want to move away from the Negative Outcomes they were now experiencing by refocusing all the attention back on directive decision-making to regain the Positive Outcomes they felt had been lost. We were using a problem-solving logic to address a polarity.

The Polarity Map makes visible the consequences of applying a problem-solving logic and either/or thinking to a polarity. You can see exactly what the consequences will be if the Positive Outcomes of *both* Poles are not achieved simultaneously. You simply cannot achieve the Greater Purpose.

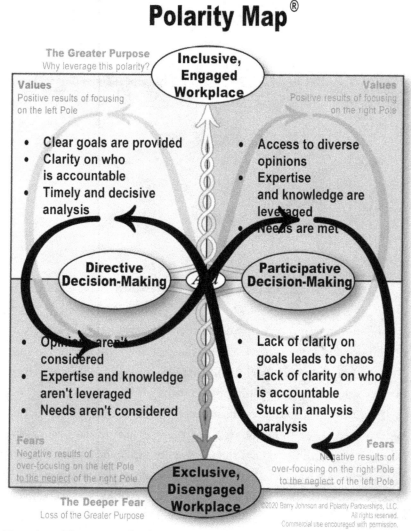

Figure 11: The Downside of Overemphasizing Participative Decision-Making

Once the respiratory therapy staff and leadership team learned about polarities, we could see the interdependency between these two decision-making styles. Now we could leverage the interdependent relationship between these Poles. How? By simultaneously implementing Action Steps from both Poles (Figure 12). This allowed us to loop back and forth, maximizing *both* directive decision-making *and* participative decision-making. Finally we could consistently reap the Positive Outcomes of both Poles and achieving the Greater Purpose of ensuring an inclusive, engaged workforce.

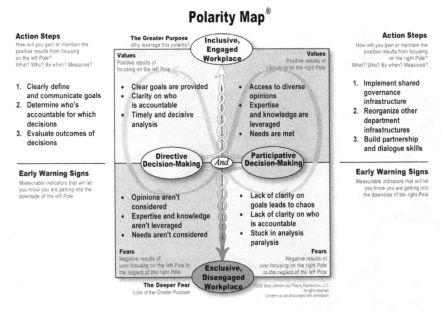

Figure 12: Directive and Participative Decision-Making Action Steps

The Action Steps are key to putting the values and ideas of the Poles into practice. These are the practical interventions you will need to implement in order to achieve the Positive Outcome of a Pole. And the only way to leverage the energy between the two Poles is to create and implement the Action Steps for both simultaneously. It is the only way to achieve the Positive Outcomes for both sides that begins a Virtuous Cycle and leads to achieving the Greater Purpose.

Doing this is what we refer to as **leveraging a polarity**.

When a polarity is leveraged well, the Infinity Loop has a substantial presence in the upper quadrants of both Poles and a negligent presence in the lower quadrant of both Poles, as you can see in Figure 11. This illustrates our sixth principal.

> **Principle 6: The only way to leverage a polarity is to simultaneously implement both Poles' Actions Steps.**

Action Steps aren't the only element to staying on track and leveraging a polarity. It's also important to recognize Early Warning Signs. These are indicators that you're starting to experience the Downside of a Pole. For example, an Early Warning Sign for the inhaling and exhaling polarity might be feeling tightness in the chest or belly. Or feeling lightheaded. If your lips are starting to turn blue, you've definitely overemphasized exhaling.

Early Warning Signs have a specific placement on the Polarity Map—to the outside of the Negative Outcomes for each Pole. (See Figure 13). In fact, the best way to identify the warning signs is to start by looking at the Negative Outcomes. For each outcome, think through what visible and measurable sign might show up.

If you look at Figure 13 and the Negative Outcomes of directive decision-making, you'll see "opinions aren't considered" at the top of the list. The Early Warning Sign that can alert us to this is statements or feelings of "No one listens to us around here." When that perception comes up in our team, we know we're too focused on directive decision-making.

When possible, it's important to choose visible and measurable Early Warning Signs. By consciously listing them next to the bottom quadrants—the Negative Outcomes—you explicitly make the connection, and they are more easily brought to your attention.

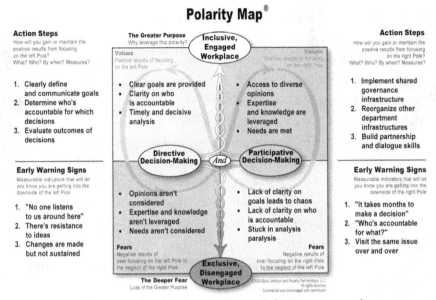

Figure 13: Early Warning Signs of the Directive and Participative Decision-Making Polarity

The Early Warning Signs act as a warning system to alert you that you have overemphasized one Pole. This helps you recognize when the Action Steps you have implemented are not achieving the intended Positive Outcome, and it allows you to make course corrections, preventing you from sliding further into the Downside of the Pole you have overemphasized.

The more diligent you are about monitoring for the Early Warning Signs, the more quickly you can evaluate and respond, thereby avoiding the Negative Consequence.

Mapping a Personal Polarity

To develop and leverage Polarity Intelligence as a leadership competency, it helps to first apply the concepts at a personal level or to a situation you frequently experience. This way, you can become familiar with the fundamental elements and principles before applying them to more complex situations at work.

You can explore and create a personal Polarity Map in a few simple steps. We refer to this as a back-of-the-napkin map because it doesn't have to be complicated. We've done it countless of times with people, right on the spot while we talk about polarities.

Grab a piece of paper—or a napkin—and simply draw a cross at the center of the paper. This will give you four quadrants. (Be sure to make it large enough that you can write in the four quadrants.) Next, write the name of one Pole on the left side of the horizontal line, and the name of the other Pole on the right size of the line. Your Greater Purpose will go at the top of the vertical line; your Deeper Fear should be written at the bottom of this line. Then, fill in the Positive Outcomes in the upper quadrants and the Negative Outcomes in the lower quadrants.

See Figure 14 for an illustration of this technique.

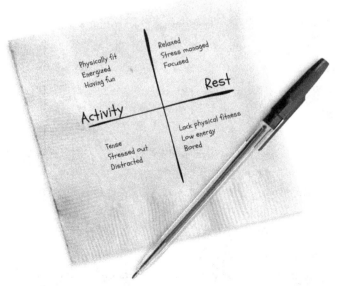

Figure 14: Back-of-the-Napkin Polarity Map

Using the back-of-a-napkin map is a great way to practice identifying polarities, naming their two Poles, and listing the Positive and Negative Outcomes of each. Eventually, you will want to create a full map where you can identify the Action Steps and Early Warning Signs—and share it with others without handing them a napkin.

Now, let's use the Work and Home Polarity as a starting point to creating your first full Polarity Map. Most leaders are acutely aware of the tension they experience between the two Poles of work and home every day.

Download the blank Polarity Map from Polarityintelligence.com, then follow the steps below to begin to create your own Work and Home Polarity Map.

Step 1: Identify the Poles. In this case, use *work* and *home*. Similar to our labels for inhale and exhale, write *work* in the oval shape on the left, and in the oval on the right, write *home*.[6]

Step 2: Clearly define each Pole. Think about work and home in a holistic way. *Work* represents any outcomes related to your job or school (whether you're a full-time student or studying part time while working), and *home* represents outcomes reflecting aspects of your personal life, such as family, friends, leisure activities, and community involvement.

Step 3: Ask yourself, "Which Pole am I drawn toward the most?" No matter what polarity you're exploring, you will always have one Pole that you prefer. There's nothing right or wrong about preferring one Pole over another. It's important to be aware of your preference, though, or else you can have a blind spot when it comes to the Downsides associated with your preferred Pole.

You also may have concerns or fears about the Downside of the opposite Pole because it represents the loss of the Positive Outcomes you value.

---

6   When filling in the elements of the map, it's important to use your own words. These are to be words that are meaningful to you as they represent your values. If you prefer to use different terms than *work* and *home*, feel free to do so. Similarly, if you're helping someone else to explore a polarity by mapping it out with them, be sure to use *their* words when filling in the elements of the map.

Step 4: Identify as many Positive Outcomes as you can for the Pole you prefer. Write these in the appropriate upper quadrant.

Step 5: Identify as many Positive Outcomes as you can for the opposite Pole. Write them in the opposite upper quadrant. Don't worry if you struggle a little with this. Identifying the Positive Outcomes of the opposite Pole may not be as easy as it was to create the list for your preference Pole, especially if you do not give this Pole as much attention. Take your time, and if you need, consult others close to you.

Step 6: Identify the Negative Outcomes you'll experience if you overfocus on the first Pole and neglect the other. List these in the left lower quadrant.

Hint: The Negative Outcomes represent the loss of the Positive Outcomes of the opposite Pole—they are often directly opposite outcomes. For example, you can look at the Positive Outcomes you identified in the upper quadrant for home, then write the opposite of each item under work, the lower left quadrant.

Step 7: Now, repeat the process and identify the Negative Outcomes you'll experience if you overfocus on the other Pole. In our example, this would be the results of an overemphasis on home while neglecting work. Hint: These will likely be opposites of the Positive Outcomes for work.

Step 8: Pause and ask, "What is my *why* for leveraging this polarity? What will I be able to achieve by intentionally giving attention to both Poles that I wouldn't be able to achieve by focusing on only one?" That is your Greater Purpose. Write it at the top of the map.

Step 9: Finally, ask, "What is the opposite of my Greater Purpose? What's at risk? What do I fear most will happen if I don't leverage this polarity well?" That is your Deeper Fear. Write it at the bottom of the map.

Leveraging a Polarity

Remember, polarities are unsolvable challenges. Unlike inhaling and exhaling, which happens naturally, most polarities require intention to ensure that the Positive Outcomes are achieved, and the invisible energy oscillates in a Virtuous Cycle toward the Greater Purpose.

Let's explore how you can leverage the Work and Home Polarity. Anytime we need to be intentional we may need time to think it through. Anytime we are learning a new skill it will take practice. *We encourage you to take time to do these steps rather than simply read through them.*

Polarities require intention to ensure the Upsides are achieved so that the invisible energy oscillates in a Virtuous Cycle toward the Greater Purpose.

Step 10: List the Action Steps. Next to each upper quadrant, list the Action Steps required for you to achieve the Positive Outcomes you've identified in your Work and Home Polarity Map.

Step 11: Identify the Early Warning Signs. Now, next to each of the bottom quadrants, list potential Early Warning Signs for each of the Negative Outcomes (or fears) you've identified for the Poles. Such Early Warning Signs would be indicators that you're starting to experience the Downside of a Pole. Identifying these signs would allow you to quickly make course corrections.

* * *

Feeling stuck? Identifying Early Warning Signs is not always easy, but don't give up. Try thinking about experiences you've had where you overfocused on one of these Poles to the neglect of the other. Also think through what comments you might hear others say to you, or things you might say to yourself—what might you be thinking, feeling, seeing, or doing when you're starting to experience the negative consequences of overfocusing on a Pole?

If you still feel stuck, ask those who know you best for input. Sometimes those closest to you see you and your patterns of behavior in ways you do not see yourself.

A Completed Work and Home Polarity Map

Having done this exercise with hundreds of leaders across North America, we have found that the Positive and Negative Outcomes leaders identify in the Work and Home Polarity are consistent. We've shown them in a completed Work and Home Polarity Map in Figure 15.

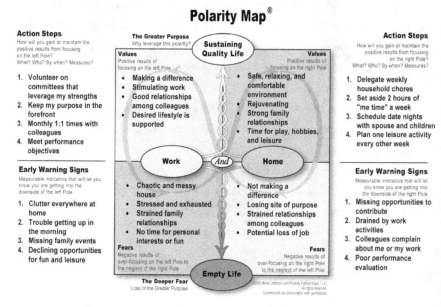

Figure 15: Complete Work and Home Polarity Map

While leveraging a polarity requires that you take simultaneous Action Steps, it doesn't require that you consistently give equal attention to each Pole all the time.

As pointed out earlier, **the goal of leveraging a polarity is to keep the energy oscillating back and forth in the upper quadrants where Positive Outcomes are being achieved. This is where dynamic balance is achieved.**

The energy between the Poles is *dynamic*, it's always moving and shifting. The goal isn't to achieve an equal balance between the two Poles.

Instead, the goal is to achieve a *dynamic balance*. This enables you to be fluid and flexible with how and where you focus your attention and actions at any point in time, while continuing to maintain the Positive Outcomes of both Poles.

Principle 7: The goal of leveraging a polarity is to achieve a state of dynamic balance and reach the Greater Purpose.

Life, business, and leadership are complex—the demands you face can shift quickly. There are times when one Pole demands more of your attention than the other. When that happens, it can leave you feeling out of balance.

The key to leveraging the polarity and achieving the dynamic balance is to give enough attention to the opposite Pole to maintain at least *some* of its Positive Outcomes, if not all.

Principle 8: When focus is heavily weighted on one Pole, you must place enough focus on the opposite Pole to at least maintain the Positive Outcomes of that Pole.

Identifying Early Warning Signs can alert you when you're overfocusing on one Pole while neglecting the other. These signs will also keep you from slipping into an either/or mindset. The Early Warning Signs will guide you to make course corrections and increase, or change, how you're attending to the opposite Pole.

Be vigilant about monitoring your Early Warning Signs. Implement your Action Steps as soon as you experience the warning signs. This will keep the energy flowing in a positive direction, toward your Greater Purpose.

Keeping your Work and Home Polarity Map in front of you will help you stay attuned. As long as you continue to work, the Work and Home Polarity will never go away. Living a quality life requires that you leverage the ongoing tension between the Poles.

How Polarities Show Up

Polarities are everywhere, and they show up in consistent ways. Knowing this can help you to identify them. Here are some examples of how they are likely showing up in your world.

Conflict

When you feel strongly about an issue while someone else in your world has a different perspective on it, both of you will hold on to what you value because you fear that what you value is at risk. This is how polarities show up as conflict. If you view the situation as either/or, you will resist considering, let alone accepting, the opposing perspective.

Remember my experience with decision-making in the respiratory therapy department? Say you value directive decision-making—like I did at the time. If your team requests to be involved in the decision-making, because they may value participative decision-making, you might fear losing the benefits of directive decision-making. (In Figure 10, we list those as clear goals being provided, clarity on accountability, and timely and decisive decision-making.)

These fears may lead you to resist your team's suggestion rather than explore and embrace it. Meanwhile, your team is likely experiencing the loss of what they value regarding participative decision-making. (In Figure 10, we list those as accessing diverse opinions, leveraging expertise and knowledge, and that their needs are met.)

The more tightly you hold on to your perspective, the more tightly they will hold on to theirs. This results in increasing tension between you and your team. And if you and your team don't see the polarity but instead treat the tension as a problem to be solved, both parties will start seeing the increasing tension as conflict.

Repetitive Problems

Problems have an end point. Polarities are ongoing. If you encounter the same problem over and over, it is likely you're actually experiencing a polarity. When you treat a polarity as a problem, you'll focus on implementing Action Steps to achieve the Upsides of only one Pole and fail to recognize that there is, in fact, another Pole.

Whether you know it's there or not, it is. And soon enough, when you experience the Downside of overemphasizing your preferred Pole, you'll look for another solution, inevitably shifting your attention to the other Pole, believing it's the answer to your problem.

That's what happened when I was looking for solutions to the challenges in the respiratory therapy department. I did a 180 and fully embraced participative decision-making as *the* solution ... until we started to face the Downside of overemphasizing that Pole.

Until you recognize that you're facing a polarity, you'll alternate your attention between the two Poles and keep trying to resolve the problem (showing up as Negative Outcomes of overfocusing on one Pole and then the other). You'll keep implementing Action Steps that only address the Pole that you see as the solution.

An example of a repetitive problem leaders often face is having the right number of great employees for the organization to function at its best. What's at play is the Recruitment and Retention Polarity. (We will provide a detailed example of this polarity in Chapter 5.)

To have enough great employees, you must retain the ones you have while also recruiting quality employees to replace those who choose to move on from your company, whatever the reason may be.

When you are able to maintain the dynamic balance between recruitment and retention, you'll experience the Upsides of both Poles. And when you're able to sustain this Virtuous Cycle, you'll reach the Greater Purpose of having an adequate supply of quality employees.

Resistance

When you find yourself being resistant to an idea, consider what you might be afraid of. More often than not, fear lurks behind resistance. We fear losing what we value.

For example, if you value stability for its consistency and predictability, then you may resist change. You'll be convinced that change will lead to inconsistency and chaos. Or if you value the freedom to choose, you may be someone who resisted being required to get the COVID vaccine. You may have clung to your freedom to choose, fearing that it was being taken from you.

When you experience resistance to a solution that someone else believes will solve a problem, it's important to ask, "What's the fear or concern regarding the solution?" Your resistance can be an indicator that there's another perspective you haven't considered, and the concern you have represents a loss of your value.

Resistance is an indicator something is missing in your approach. What's missing usually is the other interdependent Pole.

Complaints with Solutions

Polarities can also show up in the form of Negative Outcomes that lead to a complaint being voiced. However, when the complaint is presented along with a solution, in many such cases, that solution is often the contradictory perspective within a polarity. Going back to the decision-making challenges I faced years ago, here's what this looks like.

When the respiratory therapy staff complained about issues associated with *directive decision-making* in our department, I saw *participative decision-making*—the contradictory perspective—as the solution to our directive-decision making problem. So, to address the complaints, I engaged the staff in decision-making. This, I believed, would meet their desire to contribute their expertise and knowledge when we had to make decisions.

Soon enough, we experienced the Negative Outcomes of overfocusing only on participative decision-making. We experienced those Negative Outcomes not because participative decision-making wasn't the solution to our problem; it was the opposite Pole in a polarity.

As a polarity, there was no single right solution. We needed both directive *and* participative decision-making in our department.

Preferred State

There are times when your team might express a desire for things to change. They want to shift from their current undesired state to a preferred state. Rather than seeing this as a problem you'll need to solve, consider how it could be a polarity instead.

For example, your team may consist of individuals who thrive working collaboratively. That is their preferred state. It may help them be more creative, and they may come up with better results when they leverage the knowledge and skills of their teammates.

If, due to circumstances outside their control, they are forced to work from home, they may struggle working alone. They might feel disconnected from you and the rest of the team, and some may even feel ineffective working independently. This will fuel their longing to work in their desired state: *with others.*

You'll need a both/and approach—utilizing tools and resources so that working independently can be complimented by collaboration with others.

* * *

Now that you have a foundational understanding of the how the elements of a polarity work together, you can apply this knowledge to leverage the tension in any polarity you may encounter, whether in your personal life, in business, or in leadership.

Overview

Principle 1: Both Poles in a polarity are equally important.

Principle 2: Alone, neither Pole can reach the Greater Purpose.

Principle 3: When the Positive Outcomes of both Poles are achieved, the energy is positive, and it flows toward the Greater Purpose.

Principle 4: When you overemphasize or overfocus on one Pole and neglect the other, you'll experience the Negative Outcomes of the Pole you focused on.

Principle 5: The Negative Outcomes of overfocusing on one Pole lead to a loss of the Positive Outcomes of the opposite Pole.

Principle 6: The only way to leverage a polarity is to simultaneously implement both Poles' Action Steps.

Principle 7: The goal of leveraging a polarity is to achieve a state of dynamic balance and reach the Greater Purpose.

Principle 8: When focus is heavily weighted on one Pole, you must place enough focus on the opposing Pole to at least maintain the Positive Outcomes of that Pole.

Reflection Questions

1. Look at your Work and Home Polarity Map. Over the past three months, what have you been experiencing more of—the Negative Outcomes, or the Positive Outcomes? Why?

2. How well do you think you're leveraging this polarity? What would your coworkers or family say regarding how well you're leveraging this polarity?

Call to Action

- Choose one Action Step you can take to improve how you're leveraging the Work and Home Polarity, then do it.

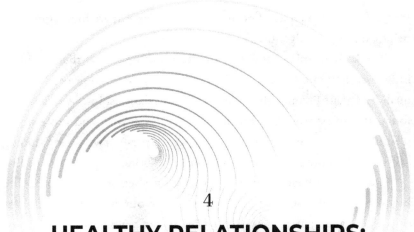

4

HEALTHY RELATIONSHIPS: AT THE HEART OF POLARITY INTELLIGENCE

*Relationships are all there is. Everything in the universe only exists
because it is in relationship to everything else. Nothing exists in isolation.
We have to stop pretending we are individuals that can go it alone.*
Margaret J. Wheatley | *Turning to One Another*

Relationships are the core of all of humanity. Your life is the outcome of relationships, and no life can be sustained without them.
The purpose of this chapter is to explore why having a healthy
relationship—first with yourself and then with others—is essential when
it comes to how you engage others on your leadership journey. Our goal

is to reveal the principles of healthy relationships that are foundational to being polarity intelligent.

Think about this. If it is true that relationships are at the core of all humanity, it is safe to say that there is a strong correlation between the quality of your life and the quality of your relationships. We have also found this to be true: You can navigate both personal and professional relationships in such a way that it honors each person's wholeness. Doing so leads to high-quality relationships and, therefore, a high quality of life.

Tracy and I have been beyond blessed when it comes to having high-quality relationships in many areas of our lives. Our relationship as business partners and best friends has taught us many lessons about healthy professional and personal relationships. We are also both blessed with great marriages, and we have been blessed to have some wonderful mentors who have been exemplars for what healthy relationships look like.

Not all of our relationships have been easy, though. When we encounter relational challenges, we see it as an invitation to take a deeper look into what's going on in our hearts, to ask why the relationship is difficult, and to examine why we might be offended or even defensive. When we pause and give it attention, it allows us to do the internal work necessary to improve the relationship or move on.

In business and leadership contexts we usually refer to these high-quality relationships as partnering relationships or empowering relationships. When it comes to Polarity Intelligence, we have chosen the term *healthy relationships* to describe the type of relationships that are critical for cultivating Polarity Intelligence in all aspects of our lives.

- Healthy relationships are relationships that are intentional and centered on a shared purpose.
- Such relationships recognize the human capacity in each person and that we are all equally responsible to achieve a shared purpose.

- They honor the need to balance the relationship with personal needs and the needs of others.
- They create trust by each being trustworthy.
- People in healthy relationships are soul-connected and bring out the best in one another.
- A healthy relationship does not mean it's a perfect relationship. Rather, it is one where each person feels good about themselves and is a better person because of the connection to another.
- In a healthy relationship you have respect for yourself *and* others. It allows all individuals to thrive.

There are also other qualities of healthy relationships that warrant a closer look.

Healthy Relationships Are Transformational

Relationships in general can be classified as either *transactional* or *transformational*. In a transactional relationship, the focus is on getting a task done. There are also relationships where the parties in the relationship merely co-exist without a shared purpose. There is no personal growth; there is simply one or more transactional interactions, and then you move on.

These transactional relationships often represent fulfilling a necessity; they are what makes the world go round. Everything from buying groceries to placing an order at a restaurant is usually accomplished through transactional relationships. There is an emphasis on getting the job done or the goal accomplished rather than on the people behind the service and their growth.

A transformational relationship, on the other hand, is one where there is a deeper connection with another person. This deep connection creates new self-awareness and changes who you both are. Due to the nature of the relationship, you commonly experience positive changes. You discover more gratitude and happiness. And you make decisions that benefit you both.

Such a relationship is highly regarded by both parties. Maintaining it requires ongoing intention as well as attention. It's good to remember that when a relationship had become transactional, you can once again nurture it into a transformational relationship.

In life and business, you don't need all relationships to be transformational, though. Both transactional and transformational relationships have their place in the world. As such, they represent a polarity. Figure 16 shows these relationships from a polarity mindset.

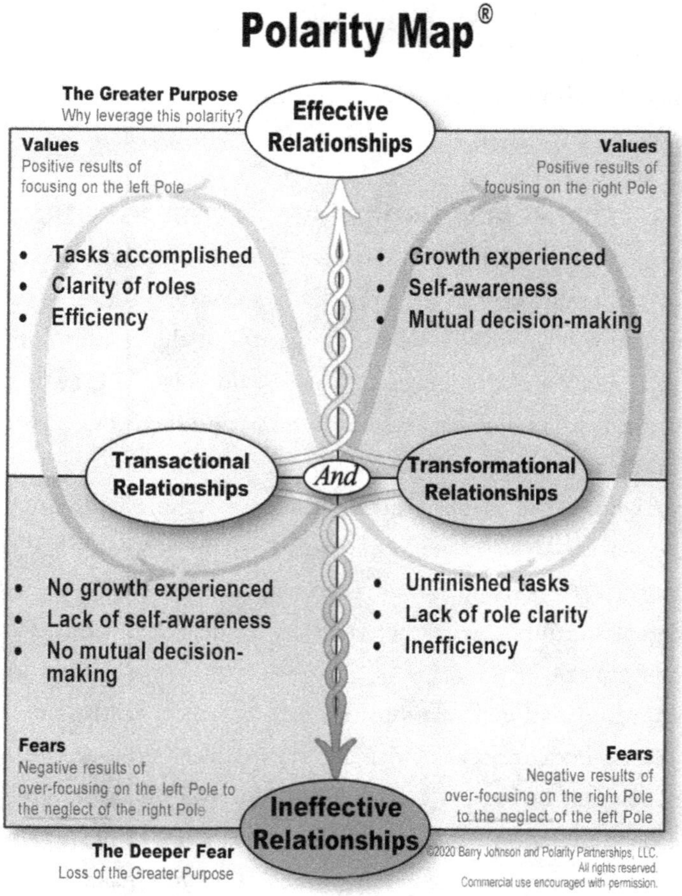

Figure 16: Transactional and Transformational Relationships Polarity Map

From this Polarity Map, you can see that both transactional and transformational relationships have Positive Outcomes (as seen in the two upper quadrants). However, if you focus more on transactional relationships to the neglect of transformational relationships, you'll experience the loss of the benefits of transformational relationships. This leads to you suffering from the Negative Outcomes of too much focus on transactional relationships.

Likewise, if you focus more on transformational relationships to the neglect of transactional ones, you'll experience the loss of the benefits of transactional relationships. You'll suffer from the Negative Outcomes of too much focus on transformational relationships.

It goes without saying that healthy relationships are, by nature, more transformational. Healthy relationships are a foundational component of Polarity Intelligence because if relationships are healthy, it makes mutual understanding, shared purpose, and leveraging polarities much easier.

Healthy Relationships Impact Culture and Economy

The nature of relationships has a tremendous impact on culture—whether at home or at work. If your relationships aren't healthy, your family and work culture won't be healthy. As a result, there is much wisdom in developing healthy relationships so you can live and work in healthy, thriving cultures where everyone is engaged in achieving a shared purpose.

Tracy and I have seen this firsthand. Both professionally and personally, we've focused on nurturing healthy relationships. Professionally, we've provided coaching and consulting to help various organizations develop healthy relationships and partnership infrastructures that create thriving work cultures.

Our experience has shown us that changes in technology, structure, or strategy do not transform the organization; people do. People make up the relationships within the organization. Hence, in our work with organizations, we support transformation at the individual level by addressing the company's core values and principles. We also address opportunities for personal and professional development that can allow for healthy relationships and a healthy culture.

The quest to create a healthy work culture crosses all professions and industries. One of the markers of a healthy culture within a company is the level of staff engagement. Gallup defines this as "involved in, enthusiastic about, and committed to their work and workplace." [7]

According to Gallup's most recent *State of the American Workplace Report,* only 33% of employees are engaged.[8] That means that two-thirds of all workers are disengaged and, therefore, less likely to be productive.

Imagine what it does to your company's bottom line when most of your employees are not involved in, enthusiastic about, or committed to their work? What does it cost you when they are not contributing to your company's or organization's success?

Gallup places the cost of lost productivity to the US economy at between $450 billion and $605 billion each year. This is because actively disengaged employees are "more likely to steal from their companies, negatively influence their coworkers, miss workdays, and drive customers away."[9]

Gallup's employee engagement survey consists of just twelve statements—seven of them have elements related to or impacted by relationships, including item ten: "I have a best friend at work." This suggests that relationships are predominant in work environments; they will contribute to your company's culture and bottom line—either positively or negatively.

All organizations face the challenge to create an engaged, collaborative, and productive work culture with sustainable Positive Outcomes. Angela Duckworth rightly points out, "Whether we realize it or not,

---

7   Gallup, Inc. 2017. *State of the American Workplace Report.* https://www.gallup.com/workplace/238085/state-american-workplace-report-2017.aspx p. 62

8   Ibid. p. 1

9   Ibid, p. 19

the culture we live in and with which we identify powerfully shapes just about every aspect of our being."[10] She goes on to explain culture as being "… the invisible psychological boundaries separating *us* from *them*. At its core, culture is defined by the shared norms and values of a group of people."[11]

Duckworth's description of culture closely aligns with how Bonnie Wesorick describes culture: the connection or disconnection of the unseen souls that exist in the workplace.

There is unquestionably an underlying *unseen* aspect to culture. Culture provides the *feel* of an organization or a home. Culture is also a *force* and, as such, it can either be an enhancer or an inhibitor to a goal or strategy. This is why Peter Drucker famously says, "Culture eats strategy for breakfast."

To emphasize the significant force of culture, I've heard many leaders add to Drucker's saying, emphasizing, "Culture eats strategy for breakfast, lunch, *and* dinner!"

You might wonder how you can best address the big challenge of unhealthy relationships and culture—both in your professional and personal lives.

At MissingLogic, we have found six guiding principles that are key to creating healthy relationships with yourself and others. Living every day by these principals not only builds positive relationships; it also enhances your capacity to lead with Polarity Intelligence. In Chapter 6, we'll take a closer look at how healthy relationships impact Polarity Intelligence.

Principles of Healthy Relationships
Principle 1: Being Intentional
Being intentional in the way that you connect with another person means that you choose to be fully present. Doing so leads to connecting

---

10 Duckworth, A. 2016. *GRIT: The Power of Passion and Perseverance.* New York: Simon & Schuster. p. 244

11 Ibid.

at an inner-being or soul level, which is foundational for developing healthy relationships.

Intentionality doesn't mean that you connect with someone to control them or to control the conversation. It is not simply listening so you can respond. Instead, it means that you purposely connect to deepen insights within yourself and the other person. If you're both fully present and you intently listen, the relationship can be healthy right from the start, and it can have significant long-term implications.

To demonstrate the life-changing power of an intentional one-on-one connection, there are few better examples than that of renowned pediatric neurosurgeon, Dr. Ben Carson. After graduating from Yale University and University of Michigan Medical School, Dr. Carson was accepted as one of only two neurosurgery residents by Johns Hopkins Hospital in Baltimore, Maryland.

In *Gifted Hands,* Dr. Carson shares how, years later, he learned that a mentor, Dr. Udvarhelyi, had vigorously advocated for his acceptance to the program. What led to this? It was the strong personal connection the two of them had made in their first meeting when Dr. Carson intentionally shared about his love for classical music, discovering that Dr. Udvarhelyi shared this passion.

Being intentional in our connection with others can happen in a single encounter yet have a ripple effect, leading to a greater good far beyond our imagination.

Intentionality also allows you to be vulnerable. Choosing to be vulnerable makes you accessible to others and reveals your true self. It also creates space for the other person to be vulnerable. This posture encourages comfort, connection, learning, and trust, and it is integral to all healthy relationships, both professionally and personally.

You may be able to recall times in your own life when the value of intention has made an impact on you. Similarly, you don't have to look far to notice how intentionality can be interrupted by something as simple as the constant buzz of a cell phone.

My husband and I witnessed this during a dinner at our favorite restaurant. There was a couple seated at a table near ours. It seemed that every time the couple connected in conversation, the woman's iPhone would buzz.

Instead of silencing her phone, she would pick it up. Her date's growing frustration was clear. We suspected he was thinking, *And who invited your iPhone on our date?*

The gentleman may have intentionally invited her to spend time together. He may have intentionally picked dinner for two. While he was probably looking forward to an evening of good conversation, possibly leading to a healthy relationship, his date seemed more committed to her phone than to him. What could have been an intimate date turned into what appeared to be an evening of frustration for the young man.

Michelle and Kevin's Sunday Check-Ins

Anyone in a committed relationship can attest to how crucial intentionality is if you want to keep your personal relationships healthy.

My husband, Kevin, and I are both entrepreneurs and leaders. We had gotten so busy during the week that it had led to our relationship and our communication becoming more transactional. This led us to feel disconnected from what was happening in each other's world and, worse yet, from each other.

Such a disconnect didn't align with our stated values of transparency and partnership, both at a family level and at a business level. Since these values are exceptionally important, once Kevin and I noticed the disconnect in 2021, we developed a weekly ritual that we call "church and check-in" or "Sunday check-in."

Each Sunday morning, we prioritize spending two hours of uninterrupted time intentionally checking in with each other. We begin by each sharing something that fed our soul that week—often an inspirational spiritual reading. We dialogue about what each of us shared, and then we switch to goals. Using the agenda below, we talk about our professional and personal goals from the previous week, we set our intentions and goals for the coming week, and end by going through our mail from the past week so it doesn't pile up.

- **Check-in** and reflection
- **Celebrate:** Review accomplishments, including work–life balance
- **Home finances:** Review account balances, budgets, bills, and anticipated expenses
- **Businesses finances:** Review current and anticipated revenue
- **Quarterly business updates:** Review each of our businesses' goals
- **Family headlines:** Updates on immediate and extended family
- **Calendars:** Review and sync our calendars for the week and touch base on upcoming commitments
- **Weekly Big 3:** Talk about each of our business and personal Big 3 goals
- **Closing prayer:** Declare intentions
- **Mail:** Go through USPS mail from the week and keep, toss, or shred

When we first started doing this, it seemed a bit odd to schedule something of this nature. But it took just a couple of Sunday check-ins for us to see how helpful it was, and we committed to keep this soulful and beneficial practice going. We even keep minutes so we can look back if we miss something. We also take a moment to post our Big 3's for the week next to our bathroom mirror so they're top of mind all week.

Our intentional time together has also shown us the value of checking in with other members of our immediate family. We now have regularly scheduled check-ins with our three grown sons and their families, as well as with my mother who was widowed in 2020.

The fruit of intentionality within our family has been deeper, healthier connections—something we are all thankful for.

Principle 2: Establishing a Shared Purpose

At a personal level, it's important that the key players in a relationship have clarity surrounding their shared purpose in their day-to-day interactions. But this also applies in professional relationships. At the highest level, this principle of coming together in pursuit of a common outcome speaks to why a business exists.

Having a shared purpose drives individuals toward a common outcome. When two or more people agree on what they see as a desired common outcome, it generates energy toward that goal. It also brings together individual purposes and their contribution to the common goal.

One example of how to facilitate this is by establishing annual goals and working through the process to break them down into quarterly or 90-day outcomes. Setting such goals makes it possible for individuals and teams to work in concert and to measure their progress along the way. What's more, everyone involved experiences the thrill of contributing and gaining momentum toward common outcomes. Ultimately, this contributes to them having a shared purpose.

Connecting Employees During the Pandemic

Like most businesses, one of our clients—a global media company—shifted to having staff work remotely during the COVID-19 pandemic. After addressing employee safety, supporting the needs of employees, and prioritizing business continuity, it became clear to the executive leadership team that employee engagement must be an even higher priority with all employees working remotely.

With a recent acquisition of another company prior to the pandemic, and the now lack of face-to-face meetings, the leadership team was concerned about the impact on team relationships and their ability to deliver their work product/services. Using the parent company's Innovation Seed Fund, they committed to fund an initiative that would increase staff engagement while working remotely.

Teams all across the company were given the opportunity to present their own innovative solutions. The winning team pitched the idea of launching a company-wide initiative called the Connect & Collaborate (C&C) Initiative. They formed a C&C Core Resource Team and included leaders and employees from across the company. This team planned a kickoff event as well as a strategy to further engage employees. They held C&C meetings where all staff could connect and build healthy relationships and get feedback on their collaborative projects.

At the C&C kickoff event, the facilitators showed Simon Sinek's TED Talk "How Great Leaders Inspire Action" to underscore the significance of starting with purpose (their *why*). Future meetings would be centered around coming together for a shared purpose.

Based on the collective input on why they were there and what purpose they thought the initiative fulfilled, they developed a C&C Company Charter to guide their efforts.

The C&C Resource Team gave regular updates to the executive leadership team and the executive sponsor. Employees reported several Positive Outcomes, including meeting people across the company whom they never would have met before, an increased sense of shared purpose, feeling like they were not alone in dealing with work and pandemic issues, and increased collaboration on shared work.

The company's intentional work to re-establish a shared purpose paid off.

Principle 3: Recognizing Equal Responsibility

Being clear on the shared purpose is one thing, recognizing that we all have equal responsibility in achieving it is another. Accepting mutual responsibility for achieving a shared purpose fuels healthy relationships, while relationships being driven by position, power, or fear drive relationships apart. Shared responsibility also allows the parties to complement one another. If one party sees that the other is having challenges, they'll step up to help reach the shared goal.

Historically, organizations tend to be more hierarchical. There is a clear chain of command and responsibilities, and directives get pushed down through the organization. This makes it more challenging for leaders to recognize the power of healthy relationships and the power of sharing equal responsibility for the shared purpose.

Supplementing a traditional hierarchical infrastructure—a vertical structure—with a council infrastructure—a horizontal structure—can yield different results. A council infrastructure creates a network of connected relationships throughout the organization. Plus, it can take on different formats to contribute to a shared purpose.

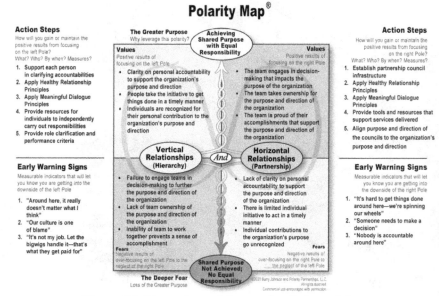

Figure 17: Hierarchy and Partnership Polarity Map

Both hierarchy and partnerships are important in any family, organization, and society. If we put a polarity lens on, the Hierarchy and Partnership Polarity is a great example how relationships within both Poles contribute to a shared purpose, regardless of roles or positions.

A closer look at this polarity reveals that, depending on how the polarity is managed, it can either uphold the principle of equal responsibility, or it can violate it. If there is an overfocus on either Pole to the neglect of the other, the healthy relationship principle of sharing equal responsibility will be at risk.

- **An overfocus on hierarchy:** Failure to engage others in decision-making, team disengagement resulting in lack of team accomplishment. Hear things like "Around here, it really doesn't matter what you think."

- **An overfocus on partnership:** Lack of clarity on personal accountability, limited individual initiative, and when individual contributions happen, they go unrecognized. Hear things like "Nobody's accountable around here."

As leaders, paying attention to this polarity, makes it easier to live out the principle of sharing responsibility for fulfilling a shared purpose. It's essential to understand the value of the contributions made by each member of the organization. It's equally important to recognize your own responsibility toward such a shared purpose.

When you can leverage hierarchy to provide resources, and at the same time intentionally partner with your employees and peers, it creates trust, teamwork, mutual respect, and momentum toward achieving the shared purpose.

Living out this principle applies equally in your personal life. With your children, intentionally supplement "Do as I say" (i.e., wearing a hierarchical parenting hat), with "How can I support you most?" (i.e., wearing a partnering parenting hat). This achieves momentum toward reaching your family's shared purpose.

Creating Equal Responsibility Through Councils

The most effective way we have seen organizations recognize equal responsibility to achieve a shared purpose and leverage the Hierarchy and Partnership Polarity is by establishing a council infrastructure.

Councils are a way to share work and leadership in an organization. Councils foster equal responsibility by engaging everyone from formal leaders to frontline employees, giving them all a voice. They bring everyone's knowledge and suggestions to the table and provide time and space for contributions.

Common Characteristics of Councils

1. Councils are led by an employee-level leader closest to the work; organizational leaders may be members of the council. In some

models, a staff leader partners with an organizational leader to head up a council.

2. Council members create one-on-one relationships with members of their department to foster healthy relationship building as well as to channel input and feedback to and from the council meetings.

3. Senior leaders keep councils abreast of organizational goals and strategic plans.

4. Each council creates their own annual goals, which further builds shared purpose. Each council also takes into consideration the organizational goals; their purpose aligns with the organizational goals as well as with the goals unique to their department or project.

5. Councils are an easy environment for applying the principles of healthy relationships and engaging in meaningful dialogue.

6. Councils complement problem-solving with leveraging polarities.

7. Councils meet regularly, often monthly. This allows opportunities to strengthen relationships and reach their intended goals.

8. Each council leader is part of a central council, linking all councils together. The goal of the central council is to share department goals and move organizational goals forward.

9. Some councils include long- and short-term shared work groups that are formed to address focused work goals.

10. Councils seek consensus on most issues with official voting reserved for decisions on leadership changes.

11. Councils celebrate their successes when goals are achieved.

By creating a model of shared leadership and connecting with employees through one-on-one relationships, councils empower employees at all levels to contribute to the organizational goals.

The council infrastructure leverages the hierarchy structure by having formal leaders as council members, and it leverages the partnership structure by having a network of connections across the organization for input, feedback, and relationships.

Principle 4: Realizing Human Capacity

This principle focuses on the potential we each hold to continually learn, grow, and evolve. When you realize your human capacity, it helps you do your part to cultivate healthy relationships in your professional and personal lives.

The great German philosopher and poet Wolfgang Goethe described the value of this principle: "Treat a man as he is, and he will remain as he is. But treat a man as he can and should be, and he will become as he can and should be."

Indeed, the gift of healthy relationships is that it not only gives you an opportunity to know yourself in a different way and to clarify your purpose, it also gives you the opportunity to help *others* along their journey.

In her cutting-edge book, *Leadership and the New Science,* Meg Wheatly suggests, "We don't know who we are until we have a relationship with another."[12] We agree, and we'd add that you also don't know your *capacity* until you're in relationship.

Think about it. Was there someone who saw leadership capacity in you before you did? We often ask this question during workshops and training sessions, and most of the time, we see heads nodding affirmatively and smiles forming as leaders remember someone who had noticed something in them that they themselves had not seen.

Within the context of healthy relationships, not only do you discover your strengths and the strengths of those closest to you, but you also

---

12 Wheatly, M. 1992. *Leadership and the New Science.* San Francisco: Berrett-Koehler Publishers, Inc.

create space for their desires, observe their unique strengths, and gain a greater sense of their capabilities.

One practical way to uncover the strengths of those around you is through Gallup's work in the field of strength-based leadership.[13] For more than a decade, we've been relying on Gallup's books, research, and assessments in this field, not only for our own development and awareness, but also with our leadership teams and clients.

When you know your top strengths and those of your team, it helps you all lean into what you are naturally good at. It also helps you appreciate what others bring to the table; seeing their capabilities fosters teamwork and allows you to make space for the best in others to come out.

Despite having vastly different strengths, neither Tracy nor I ever feel less than the other. Instead, we are grateful that our strengths complement each other so we both deliver on our full capacity in serving our clients.

Tracy's Education Journey: A Story of Realizing Human Capacity

This is my (Tracy's) personal story of living this principle of a healthy relationship as I pursued multiple degrees over the last thirteen years.

When I graduated with an associate degree as a respiratory therapist, I was happy simply using my training in that field. Not too long into my career, I had the honor of working under the leadership of Bonnie Wesorick (as told in Chapter 1). This opened the doors to leading salient work at our hospital group, helping to co-create healthy work cultures and advancing interprofessional collaborative practices across the country. I *loved* doing that.

---

13   Roth, T. and Conchie, B. 2009. *Strength-Based Leadership.* Gallup Press.

While people told me that I didn't need an additional degree to do what I was doing, I began to sense that that there were things that I could only gain from a formal education. So, while working full-time, I returned to school. After earning a bachelors and then a master's degree, I had a clear vision for what I wanted to contribute to the world through MissingLogic.

I knew I had it in me to learn how to pursue a PhD so I could demonstrate the outcomes of my and Michelle's work. In 2017, leveraging my support systems and strengths, I embarked on the journey of getting a doctorate. I did well, maintaining a 4.0 grade-point average.

But two years into the program, I received an email from the program chair that she had to give me an F for the quarter because my committee chair had reported I had not made any progress. I was shocked! There had been no communication from my committee to indicate I wasn't meeting standards. I called the program chair as soon as I could, and she shed some light on the situation. Together, we set up a plan to follow up with my committee.

At the time, I was also in a group coaching program. We happened to have a group call before I followed up with my committee. When I shared my disappointment, I broke down. "What if this dream doesn't happen? What about all the work I had already done?" I shared between tears.

"You're attached to the outcome," my coach said, "and you have to trust and let that go. You have no control over what they're going to do…" So, that's what I did. After meeting with my committee, they decided not to change their decision and shortly thereafter my entire dissertation committee quit.

I was at a crossroads. I did some deep reflection on my part in the experience and realized that I had not chosen the right people to support me with my dissertation. But what was I supposed to do next, and what did this all mean? Did I even *want* to keep going?

Most importantly, I wondered if I had the capacity to keep going. I posed this question to my program chair—she believed I did. I asked those in my support system the same, and they too believed I had it in me to complete the program.

So, I chose a new topic, new committee chair, and new committee members. And I started over.

On June 3, 2022, I walked across the stage to receive my PhD. My husband, Jerry, was at my side, and Michelle and her husband were in the audience. It's a moment forever etched in my mind. I'll be forever grateful for the advice from my coach, my committee, and my support system for seeing me through this step of my journey.

Here's what I learned about realizing human capacity:

- Trust that what's happening is happening *for* you, not against you.
- Pay attention to what a challenging experience teaches you about yourself. For me it led to a huge transformational leap, not just as a scholar, but as a human being.
- Have faith that others involved in the process will also learn what they need to from the experience.
- Lean into your strengths. One of my strengths is that I'm a learner. Through this difficult process, I needed to lean into that strength in order to move forward without putting unnecessary expectations on myself.
- Surround yourself with a cheer squad who already knows your human capacity. And fill yourself up with positive stories and affirmations.

Principle 5: Balancing Relationship with Self and Others

To form a healthy relationship, you first need to be healthy yourself. And that starts with being balanced within yourself. Only then can you bring your full self to the relationship, connect at a soul level, and do your part to contribute to your shared purpose.

Achieving personal balance encompasses your ability to self-organize and keep a balance within your body, mind, and spirit. When you're balanced, you feel grounded, whole, and motivated. But when you're out of balance with yourself, you feel out of sorts, scattered, and unmotivated.

No one can achieve personal balance for anyone else. It's work that each person has to do by intentionally pursuing self-discovery and continuous learning.

The personal balance of each person influences the balance of a team—a dynamic seen in the Relationship with Self and Relationship with Others Polarity. This is an especially important Polarity for leaders to leverage. You must constantly monitor how well you're experiencing the Positive Outcomes of personal balance, as well as the Positive Outcomes of balance with others.

Recognizing that your relationship with self and with others are equally important helps you to prioritize your commitment to self—only then can you show up as your best self in relationship with others too. Teams can thrive when organizations prioritize this polarity.

Strategies for Balancing Relationship with Self and Others

Both Tracy and I have built into our lives the practice of having a morning routine. It has helped us live out this principle. We start our days early (between 4:30 and 5:30 a.m.) and complete one or more of the following activities to get balanced within our own body, mind, and spirit:

- Practice silence and meditation
- Reflect and journal
- Review vision, purpose, and goals
- Review the day's schedule and visualize the day

- Schedule personal time as needed
- Identify the weekly and daily Big 3 goals
- Do some physical exercise

To be in healthy relationship with each other as business partners and friends, we have intentionally committed to four key practices:

- Have regular check-ins
- Schedule together time for the business and as friends
- Follow the principles of healthy relationships
- Coach and support one another

Principle 6: Being Trustworthy

There can be no healthy relationship without trust. But which comes first, being trustworthy or extending trust to the other? We would argue it's the first. If you aren't trustworthy, how can you trust others?

How do you become trustworthy, though? You choose to be reliable and worthy of trust regarding things that matter most. To do that, you must learn to trust yourself.

How do you learn to trust yourself? Say what you are going to do, and then do what you said. It may sound simple, but we all know that it's not always easy.

The good news is that you can learn and improve whenever you find yourself falling short. In *Dare to Lead*, Brené Brown discusses the basics of self-trust and areas in your life that may need improvement. She offers this strategy: "Remember one of the founding concepts of this part: Trust is built in small amounts. If you struggle with reliability, make small and doable promises to yourself that are easy to fulfill, until you get the flywheel of reliability going again."[14]

Being trustworthy takes inner work. It requires going deep within yourself, knowing which values and principles you stand on, and then living by those every day—one small step at a time.

---

14 Brown, B. 2018. *Dare to Lead*. Vermilion

As you grow in being trustworthy, you can extend trust to others and build healthy relationships. Commit to grow in these trust-building behaviors:

- You are transparent, neither withholding information nor speaking half-truths and lies.
- You don't speak for another. Instead, you let others speak for themselves.
- You don't seek to "get buy-in" from others. Instead, you leverage dialogue skills to uncover perspectives and achieve shared purpose. (More about that in the next chapter.)
- You show respect by expressing appreciation for contributions to the shared purpose and for work well done.
- You don't try to fix or rescue others. Rather, you challenge and coach one another.
- You aren't quick to give answers. Instead, you ask questions so you can find better answers together.
- You own your actions and don't blame others, understanding that we all make choices and those choices shape our environment.
- You fulfill your commitments.
- You are committed to ongoing learning. Instead of seeing mistakes as failure, you embrace them as learning trials and experiences.
- You embody the change you want to see in the world, and you do so sooner rather than later.

Lessons from Leaders Who Inspire Trust

In a *Harvard Business Review (HBR)* article titled "The Connection Between Employee Trust and Financial Performance,"[15] Stephen Covey and Doug Conant share powerful lessons about trust. In the

---

15 Covey, M.R. and Conant, D.R. "The Connection Between Employee Trust and Financial Performance." *Harvard Business Review.* July 18, 2016.

article they describe how Conant's number one mission in the remarkable turnaround of the Campbell Soup Company was to inspire trust.

The authors identified three trust-building keys Conant used to activate the Virtuous Cycle of continuously improved performance and confidence: declaring intent, demonstrating respect, and delivering results.

Conant lived the healthy relationship principle of being intentional, and he verbally shared that intention with his team. Next, he demonstrated the principle of being trustworthy by being respectful and delivering results.

The *HBR* article reveals the significance trust can have on the bottom line. Covey and Conant cite research from *Fortune* that showed "trust between managers and employees is the primary defining characteristic of the very best workplaces," and that companies with high levels of trust "beat the average annualized returns of the S&P 500 by a factor of three."[16]

The authors further underscore how important trust is for leaders by stating:

While few leaders would argue against the idea that trust is necessary for building elite performance, not nearly enough realize the height of its importance, and far too many disregard trust-building as a "soft" or "secondary" competency. But in our joint experience, we've learned that trust is the one thing that changes everything. It's not a nice to have; it's a must have.

Without it, every part of your organization can fall, literally, into disrepair. With trust, all things are possible—most importantly: continuous improvement and sustainable, measurable, tangible results in the marketplace.[17]

---

16   Ibid.
17   Ibid.

In other words, being trustworthy is the foundation for every other possibility.

Overview

Healthy relationships are a foundational component of Polarity Intelligence. Below is a summary of each principle of healthy relationships.

1. **Being Intentional:** You have a choice to be 100% present with another person and connect at a soul level.

2. **Establishing a Shared Purpose:** The relationship centers around coming together for a common goal.

3. **Recognizing Equal Responsibility:** The relationship is driven by accepting mutual responsibility in achieving the shared purpose.

4. **Realizing Human Capacity:** There is potential in oneself and others to continuously learn, grow, and evolve.

5. **Balancing Relationship with Self and Others:** Achieve a dynamic balance between self and others to achieve a shared purpose.

6. **Being Trustworthy:** Know that personal trustworthiness precedes a trusting relationship with others.

Lacking the ability to be in healthy relation with yourself and others will impede your ability to lead with Polarity Intelligence.

Reflection Questions

1. What value do you place on having healthy relationships?

2. Identify 3-5 key relationships in your life—both professionally and personally—that would benefit from applying the principles of healthy relationships.

3. How well do you demonstrate trustworthiness to those you identified above?

4. Which principles do you excel at today?

5. Which principles do you need to work on the most?

Call to Action

- Put a plan together on how to establish and maintain a balanced relationship with yourself first.
- Set an intention as you engage with others. Look in their eyes and make a conscious choice to connect at a soul level. See beyond their physical form.
- Notice whether there is a shared purpose among your key relationships, either named or unnamed.
- Show your appreciation to team members who have demonstrated work well done and made contributions toward the shared purpose.
- Identify team or family members with untapped or under-tapped capacities. Create steps to support them to learn, grow, and evolve.

5

GAINING INSIGHT AND UNDERSTANDING THROUGH MEANINGFUL DIALOGUE

Dialogue is the fundamental skill of our time.
Darren Gold | *Thrive Global*

There is one more component that you need in your quest to become polarity intelligent: meaningful dialogue. By using meaningful dialogue, you can create a place of safety from where you can explore polarities and engage others so, together, you can learn how to employ your different perspectives to serve a Greater Purpose.

In the previous chapters, we introduced you to the elements and principles of polarities, opening the door for you to acquiring a polarity mindset. You learned how polarities work and how you need healthy relationships so you can reach the Greater Purpose represented by a polarity. By now, you also understand that in order to cultivate Polarity Intelligence, you need both a polarity mindset and healthy relationships.

In this chapter, we'll explain what exactly meaningful dialogue is, including the principles of meaningful dialogue. We'll also provide you with examples of why this is an essential skill to use to diagnose and explore polarities.

Why Meaningful Dialogue?

Dialogue has been a core part of our transformational work for decades. Early on, its importance became very clear. To hold two opposing views, or polarities, and to be able to effectively explore them with yourself and others, an effective leader must understand the nature of dialogue. They must also possess the necessary dialogue skills to guide their teams through this critically important learning.

Meaningful dialogue is a specific way of communicating and learning together. Through dialogue we gain deep understanding and generate shared meaning. It begins with setting intention and creating a safe container for psychological safety and exploration. It also requires active listening and awareness, advocacy and inquiry, candor and diplomacy, plus silence and reflection.

For Tracy and me, our first exposure to dialogue emerged from the work we did in the 1990s with healthcare systems. Over the next thirty years, we explored and adopted the discipline of team learning through dialogue and the capacity of others to suspend assumptions and enter into what author Peter Senge and others refer to as "thinking together."[18]

---

18 Senge, P., Roberts, C., Ross, R., Smith, B.., and Kleiner, A. 1994. *The Fifth Discipline Fieldbook*. Currency Doubleday

We observed and studied other industries that were willing to adopt and apply dialogue in their cultures with the intention of creating what Senge refers to as "learning organizations"[19] along with creating collaborative partnerships at work.[20]

Under the guidance of our colleagues Bonnie Wesorick and Laurie Shiparski, who led the efforts of designing a strategy to teach and practice dialogue skills in healthcare settings,[21] we were blessed to grow in our mastery of dialogue skills.

Based on these insights from our expansive and deep experience, we will share our observations, and in this chapter answer the question: Why is dialogue an essential skill for Polarity Intelligence?

What is Meaningful Dialogue?

The word *dialogue* comes from the Greek *dialogos,* with *dia* meaning through, and *logos* being the meaning.

By using dialogue, meaning is being passed through (or among) two or more people. This allows participants to access to a larger pool of meaning that they would not have been able to access individually.[22] Herein lies the beauty of dialogue: it helps you to go beyond your individual understanding.

Through dialogue, you gain insights you cannot reach alone. As such, dialogue teaches you how you can *learn* through conversation so you can gain diversity of thought—a requisite for meaningful dialogue.

For years, I (Michelle) have had a magnet on my refrigerator that reads, "Where there is understanding, there is love." To me, this saying

---

19   Senge, P. 1990. *The Fifth Discipline: The Art and Practice of the Learning Organization.* Currency Doubleday

20   Ellinor, L. and Gerard, G. 1998. *Dialogue: Rediscover the Transforming Power of Conversation.* John Wiley & Sons.

21   Wesorick, B. and Shiparski, L. 1997. *Can the Human Being Thrive in the Workplace? Dialogue as a Strategy of Hope.* Practice Field Publishing

22   Bohm, D. 1989. *On Dialogue.* David Bohm Seminars

represents the power of dialogue. Through dialogue, you can gain deep understanding and generate shared meaning in such a way that it feels like love. This process and the sense of connection with others can be a profound experience.

Dialogue is not the only form of conversation, though. Other forms include discussion, deliberation, and debate.

- The root of *discussion* is the same as those of *percussion* and *concussion*. As such, when you discuss something, you effectively break the topic into parts to achieve a goal. You'll often spot discussion rather than a true dialogue happening when a conversation is being pushed to closure or when it becomes narrowly focused on one aspect.

- *In deliberation,* you tend to weigh out an issue or situation. One way you might deliberate in conversation is when you create a list of pros and cons. While it can help shed light on the benefits and risks of the issue being discussed, the act of deliberating limits the creation of other alternatives, and it limits creativity.

- *Debate* is about justifying and defending your point of view. When debating, you're more likely to hang on to your point of view so tightly that your knuckles turn white, saying whatever it takes to get the other person or persons to see your side of things.

When it comes to polarities, you neither use discussion, deliberation, nor debate. Instead, using meaningful dialogue is central to recognizing polarities, deepening understanding, and transcending personal biases.

Using dialogue goes beyond Polarity Intelligence, though. For you to grow your effectiveness as a leader, you *must* learn to engage in meaningful dialogue. Mastering this skill includes embracing five principles of meaningful dialogue.

Principles of Meaningful Dialogue

For more than three decades, we've used and taught the principles of dialogue to leaders in our workplace, at client sites, in communities, and to families. When we started MissingLogic, one of the commitments we made was to walk our talk, to practice what we teach our clients. That includes having a continuous practice and mastery of dialogue.

We have identified five principles of meaningful dialogue. Before we dive into the details, let's look at an overview of each principle and its key characteristics.

Principles of Meaningful Dialogue

1. **Setting Intention and Creating Psychological Safety**
   - Have a clear intention and share it with others; this is the first step in creating a safe container for dialogue.
   - Be willing to create a safe place, to be clear on what you desire from the heart, and to be influenced, thus making it possible to achieve shared understanding.
   - Welcome the voice of others in an open and authentic way to create an environment that is safe for interpersonal risk-taking.

2. **Actively Listening and Being Aware**
   - Be willing to learn through intense listening to yourself and others rather than to analyze, prove, compete, judge, rescue, fix, or blame.
   - Suspend assumptions while listening to others.
   - Pay attention to verbal and non-verbal communication, including emotions.

3. **Balancing Advocacy and Inquiry**
   - Be willing to share non-scripted thinking and what is behind that thinking, with the intention of exposing—not defending—it.

- Be willing to ask questions that dig deeper, uncover insights, and provide new learning.
- Be aware whether you prefer advocacy or if you prefer inquiry so you can balance the two during conversation.

4. **Leveraging Candor and Diplomacy**
   - Be willing to speak openly and frankly, with honest beliefs or perceptions, *and to* speak with sensitivity toward the recipients of the message.
   - Recognize that both candor and diplomacy are important for meaningful conversation and achieving a shared understanding.

5. **Inviting Silence and Reflection**
   - Be willing to reflect on lessons learned through personal awareness and unspoken words.
   - Recognize the power of self-reflection as well as group reflection to reveal wisdom and provide new learning.

Principle 1: Setting Intention and Creating Psychological Safety

The first principle of meaningful dialogue is to begin by setting an intention for the conversation so you can tap into the wisdom of meaning flowing through conversation.

Being clear about your intention starts with being clear about what's in your heart regarding the matter at hand and all parties involved. Before you enter into a conversation, ask yourself, "What is my intention with *this* conversation? How can I assure that all parties experience psychological safety,[23] feel heard and trusted, and feel like they have a place at the table?"

If your intention is indeed to deepen understanding around a topic and to have meaningful conversation where everyone is psychologically

---

23   More about psychological safety later in this section.

safe, simply acknowledge your intention—especially if you're concerned that it may be misinterpreted.

In their best-selling book, *Crucial Conversations*, Kerry Patterson and his colleagues make the case that if you cannot get yourself right, you'll have a hard time getting dialogue right.[24] In other words, if you don't understand your heart in a matter, you cannot communicate clearly.

Without clarity on your intention, it can be easy to resort to unhealthy communication patterns from the past, including using a discussion, deliberation, or debate. Intention also opens the space for shared meaning or understanding. It is key to creating psychological safety.

What is psychological safety? According to Harvard Business School professor and author, Amy Edmondson, "[it] is a belief that one will not be punished or humiliated for speaking up with ideas, questions, concerns, or mistakes."[25] In other words, creating psychological safety invites people to share their thoughts without being concerned about being judged.

Google conducted a two-year study of 180 teams to determine what are the most important traits of successful teams; they found psychological safety to be the most important component. Google's study, named Project Aristotle, determined that when feeling psychologically safe, team members are more likely to take risks and to be vulnerable with each other. [26]

Risk-taking and vulnerability are expressed through communication, and learning to use dialogue skills can open the door to both. Dialogue invites attention to the whole, not just the parts. It allows you to con-

---

24 Patterson, K., Grenny, J., McMillan, R., and Switzler, A. 2002. *Crucial Conversations: Tools for Talking When Stakes Are High.* McGraw-Hill

25 Edmondson, A.C. 2019. *The Fearless Organization: Creating Psychological Safety in the Workplace for Learning, Innovation and Growth.* Wiley: Hoboken, p. 8

26 https://bit.ly/AristotleGoogle

nect the dots, invite others in, welcome diverse perspectives, gain collective insights, and create shared meaning among every participant. It also allows you to generate new ideas.

True dialogue is based on an underlying assumption that every person around the table has wisdom that you don't. Acknowledging this truth unlocks the magic of learning from one another.

But again, you cannot tap into the wisdom of others unless you're clear on your intentions and create psychological safety for everyone around the table.

Tips for Creating Dialogue by Setting Intention and Creating Psychological Safety

- Gain clarity and declare your intention *before* beginning the conversation.
- Visualize turning on a light switch as a metaphor for setting your intention.
- Begin the conversation by stating your intention to explore without judgment.

Implications for Polarity Intelligence

Having an intention to honor each person and their perspectives creates a safe place to uncover and appreciate the Positive Outcomes of each Pole of a polarity so you can achieve the Greater Purpose. It also invites you to be vulnerable regarding fears and what's at stake if one Pole has more emphasis than the other.

If you're in a position of power, people around you may be sitting in the Downside of your preference Pole. When power becomes *power over*, you cannot leverage the polarity. When this occurs, the natural tension between the Poles will be seen as resistance.

But when people see what they value is being supported, and there's a desire to prevent what they fear, it minimizes resistance.

Using Polarity Intelligence with a Church Congregation

Pauline was a business executive skilled at managing polarities in her corporate leadership role. She was also active in her local congregation of the Reformed Church in America (RCA), where she was ordained to serve as a deacon. In that role, Pauline would also serve on the consistory, a body that governs the life and ministry of an RCA congregation. The consistory is made up of the pastor, elders, and deacons. These three offices are mutually supportive and accountable.

Not long into Pauline's role as a deacon, the pastor left. The elders and deacons were charged to search for a new pastor. As they began defining the characteristics they desired in a new pastor, Pauline found it interesting that many of the characteristics were unipolar. She noticed that her colleagues were leaning toward the opposite Pole of what the previous pastor had represented.

For example, the former pastor had been good at *focusing on the congregation*, so the elders and deacons wanted someone who was good at *looking beyond the congregation*.

He was good at *preaching*, so they wanted someone who was good at *teaching*.

And he was good at *connecting locally* within their community, so they wanted someone who was good at *connecting globally*.

With her understanding of Polarity Intelligence, Pauline knew they needed someone who would be good at focusing on the congregation *and* looking beyond the congregation, someone who could preach *and* teach, and someone who was active locally *and* globally.

Pauline also knew that simply telling the others about the importance of their next pastor having the characteristics of both

Poles would not be enough. She would need to communicate these new ideas in a way that would lead to greater understanding. Doing so would require that she engage in meaningful dialogue.

Ahead of their next meeting, Pauline requested time on the agenda. She shared from her heart what her intention was—that she cared about their charge and the outcome of the process. Wanting everyone to feel safe enough to explore new ideas, Pauline used the example of the Inhale and Exhale Polarity to teach them the value of a both/and perspective, something she had learned in her corporate role.

Pauline pointed out areas where the character traits the group had identified appeared to be leaning toward one Pole only. She reminded them that the goal (their Greater Purpose) was to have a church that would thrive under the leadership of a new pastor, and that creating a more balanced profile would be an important step toward reaching that goal. Next, she set the stage for meaningful dialogue regarding their insights.

Following their dialogue, the consistory adjusted the candidate profile before handing it over to the search committee. In the end, they all felt good about the candidate that was chosen based upon them using Polarity Intelligence.

Not only did Pauline have the courage to speak up, but the way she did so—sharing her intention and creating psychological safety—led to a successful outcome.

Principle 2: Actively Listening and Being Aware

There can be no dialogue without listening. Good listening includes the awareness of others in the conversation space—including being aware of their emotions and body language. To engage in good dialogue, you also have to pay attention to what is not being said. To effectively read between the lines, practice being in the moment during a meaningful dialogue so that you may heighten your awareness of all that is happening.

This awareness is not only about focusing on what others are saying or not saying. In fact, it starts with being self-aware. Before you can be effective in listening to others, you will need to quiet the conversation going on in your own mind. To do so, start by setting the intention to be present and suspend assumptions.

Judging self or others can distract your mind from deep listening. This can cause you to become either defensive or competitive. Instead of judging, practice deep listening as an expression of deep respect and acceptance of yourself and the other. This requires effort as you become aware of your own listening skills.

You may think you know how to listen. After all, you've been told to listen since you were a child. Listen to your parents. To your teachers. To your friends. But as you have grown as a leader, you will have come to know the value and importance of listening well to your teams and colleagues, not to mention your spouse. Your company may have even offered you training on listening. This is not the type of listening required when it comes to meaningful dialogue.

Effective dialogue requires different listening skills than any other type of listening you may have been exposed to. It requires that you do not analyze, judge, or blame. It also requires that you keep from competing, proving, rescuing, or fixing.

Instead, listening for effective dialogue requires a willingness to learn by being completely present and focused on what someone else is saying through spoken and unspoken messaging. It requires listening at a much deeper level so you can take in all the information. Listening like *this* leads to understanding.

And the reason so few people practice this kind of listening is that it's harder than it seems. You can learn how to master this skill, though. And as you practice listening with intentionality, as you practice awareness during a conversation, you will become more open to new ideas that you can add to the pool of shared understanding.

The reason why this is challenging is because your brain naturally steps in when you hear something that you think puts the ideas you hold at risk. Your brain makes you want to stand up for what you think is right.

Wharton professor and thought leader Judith Glaser describes this as an amygdala hijack, where the amygdalae at the center of your brain take over by searching for what you already believe instead of listening to others. Once hijacked, your higher brain goes offline for as long as seventeen minutes, during which time it's unavailable for the complex cognitive tasks that relationships require.[27]

By intentionally listening without judging, you avoid this.

To be a leader skilled at meaningful dialogue, it's imperative that you not only know how polarities work but also become a student of the art of listening. And as you grow in this area, you can teach it to your team.

Tips for Creating Dialogue by Actively Listening and Being Aware

- Set your intention to listen deeply.
- Give your full attention. Make eye contact, pay attention to non-verbal cues, listen without thinking of your response. Above all, refrain from multitasking.
- Pay attention to your areas of comfort and discomfort while listening. Are there areas you feel tension? Are you picking up the other person's discomfort?
- Reflect on what you heard, then validate as needed.
- Ask questions to gain more clarity.

---

27   Glaser, J. E. 2014. *Conversational Intelligence: How Great Leaders Build Trust and Get Extraordinary Results.* Bibliomotion, Inc.

Implications for Polarity Intelligence

Listening in dialogue is not listening for the purpose of fixing a problem. As mentioned in Chapter 2, problem-solving can be the leader's Achilles heel and often is rooted in being trained to "listen to fix."

Polarity Intelligence invites you to listen in such a way that you welcome the voice of the other. This will allow you to discern what problems and/or polarities are present.

But you have to listen to yourself first and then to others, so when it comes to leveraging a polarity, you are aware of your natural preference Pole.

In dialogue, listen for discovery rather than listening to fix or listening for answers, as such listening practices will cause you to miss the opportunity to reveal the presence of polarities.

Are You Really Listening?

Several years ago, I (Michelle) attended a seminar for master dialogue facilitators on how to introduce dialogue within an organization. The event also focused on the role of active listening during dialogue. Growing in this area was crucial in my work of leading organizational change.

My colleagues and I were exposed to several exercises that revealed how often we don't *actually* listen to others even though we *think* we're listening. We discovered how often we simply listened on the surface, missing what was shared while we were thinking of a multitude of other things.

On the final morning of this training, while getting my children ready so I could drop them off at daycare, I was thinking about the day ahead and the meetings I had to lead at the end of the event. At the same time, I realized my car keys weren't where I always put them.

I was searching for my car keys when my husband, Kevin, shared some important details about picking up the children later in the day and our family dinner plans. While walking around the house searching for my keys, I kept calling out, "Keep talking, I'm listening. ... Yup, keep talking, I'm listening. ... OK, keep talking, I'm listening."

No matter how many times I said I was listening, I really wasn't. I was oblivious of what my husband had said—and here I'd just spent several days learning about how important it was to actively listen when another person is speaking to you!

Once I realized this, I went to Kevin and apologized. I looked directly into his eyes and said, "Now, what were you saying to me?"

This simple incident had a profound impact on me. It helped me to realize how often I *think* I'm listening—even *say* I am listening—when, in fact, I'm not. It also illustrates how listening and being aware is a critical meaningful dialogue principle for both work and home.

Principle 3: Balancing Advocacy and Inquiry

Balancing advocacy and inquiry in meaningful dialogue requires that you become aware of when to use advocacy (openly sharing) and when to use inquiry (asking questions) to uncover insights.

Advocacy in dialogue is about sharing your knowledge, your thoughts, and your feelings for the purpose of exposing it—not defending it. It's not about your expertise and role as a leader. As with other areas of growth, advocacy begins by listening to yourself first and then engaging in dialogue by voicing those thoughts.

Advocacy shows a willingness to be vulnerable enough to share your thinking as well as how you came to think that way. It calls for you and every person involved in the conversation to bring their unique voice to the table. Dialogue provides conditions that teach you to appreciate advocacy, to welcome diversity, and to not see diversity as conflict. As such, one outcome of advocacy is that it allows you to know yourself better.

Inquiry, on the other hand, means you don't know the answer to the question. Through inquiry you can gain insight, learn new information, and grow in understanding—just like you did as a child when you asked questions to learn and grow. As an adult, though, you may have lost sight of this as an important growth tool.

Inquiry comes from the Latin word that means to see within. Inquiry, along with reflection, brings clarity. As you master the art of inquiry, you will realize that generating questions around a specific issue can broaden your thinking and expose the polarities associated with it.

When you're feeling uncertain or you're feeling tension during a conversation, a good rule of thumb is to dive into inquiry. As the thirteenth-century Persian poet Rumi famously said, "Look for the answer within your question."

Inquiry is an invitation to tap the wisdom of another. While practicing inquiry, it's important to invite *all* possibilities and resist the temptation to accept what you might consider to be the right answer too soon. If you don't, the answers can be limiting, even unipolar.

Whether you're struggling with polarities personally or at work, practice balancing advocacy and inquiry as a critical skill for identifying polarities.

Tips for Creating Dialogue by Balancing Advocacy and Inquiry

- Be willing to be vulnerable by sharing your perspective and your thinking behind your perspective, that is, how you came to think that way.
- Be willing to share your preferred Pole and why you prefer it.
- With genuine curiosity, ask questions.
- When uncertain where to go next in the conversation, dive into inquiry.
- Ask more questions.

Implications for Polarity Intelligence

Inquiry is the most powerful way to uncover polarities. At the same time, as you become comfortable with advocacy, you learn to share your Pole preferences and rationale for those preferences. Your preference Pole typically is your blind spot, so it's critical that you lead with inquiry. The stronger you value your preference Pole, the harder it is to recognize its Downside, which further emphasizes the need for inquiry.

Using Polarity Intelligence, you'll also know to honor the whole picture and the absolute need for both Poles to achieve the Greater Purpose.

A New Lens for Recruitment and Retention

Carol is an experienced leader who had been working as a consultant with a healthcare organization on the West Coast. She was trained in recognizing and managing polarities. The organization where she worked was experiencing a staffing issue, something that is often looked at as a problem to be solved.

Staffing in healthcare is indeed a problem, but it also represents the Recruitment and Retention Polarity, among others. To assure sustainable staffing solutions, Carol knew that the Recruitment and Retention Polarity would need to be leveraged.

She also knew it would be important to uncover the experience of the organization she was consulting with insofar as their staffing challenges and successes with this polarity. To do so, she would need to balance advocacy and inquiry to learn all she could during her conversations with her client.

Carol shared her ideas and her thinking behind those ideas. In doing so, she provided advocacy and, through inquiry, invited the client to share their ideas. This would allow them to create common understanding together before conducting a staffing forecast analysis.

Carol brought groups of managers and directors together, and they were intentional about fostering open dialogue and shared learning. In doing so, Carol was able to tap the realities of the organizations.

Throughout the process, Carol was continually balancing advocacy with inquiry so she could learn from the managers and directors. She did this by asking, for example, about what they had done in the past that had worked and not worked. She also inquired how they had developed specialized staffing teams as a recruitment strategy.

Carol and the client were able to learn much from mutual sharing (advocacy) and from asking genuine questions (inquiry). This resulted in the organization being more strategic in managing and leveraging the Recruitment and Retention Polarity.

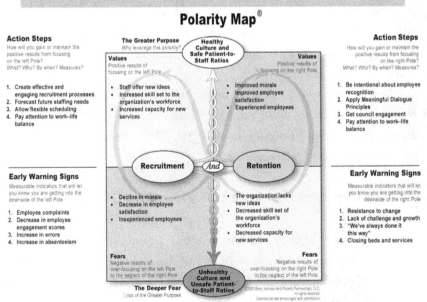

Figure 18: The Recruitment and Retention Polarity Map

Principle 4: Leveraging Candor and Diplomacy

Leveraging candor and diplomacy assures that you tap into the collective wisdom of everyone present so nothing is withheld from the shared or common pool of meaning. This principle entails expressing your beliefs and perspectives with honesty, clarity, style, and grace. It requires you to be true to your values and beliefs, yet sensitive toward the recipient(s) of the message.

This is a polarity. (You can see the Candor and Diplomacy Polarity Map in Figure 19). Candor sits on the left. Its Positive Outcomes can be summarized as openness and frankness. Diplomacy sits on the right. Its Positive Outcomes ultimately mean a message is delivered with sensitivity so it can be heard with respect. You need to practice both for effective communication.

Which is your preferred Pole—candor, or diplomacy? Do you tend to want to get right to the point and have little trouble with sharing your beliefs with others? Or do you tend to be concerned about how you express your perspective so you don't come across as insensitive? It is important to reflect on the preference and natural focus we bring with us when we communicate.

Leveraging both candor and diplomacy invites meaningful dialogue by creating space for both parties through mutual respect. Doing so assures that the conversation is meaningful, all parties can learn, and you can achieve shared understanding.

Tips for Creating Dialogue by Leveraging Candor and Diplomacy

- Be aware of your preference Pole and communication style. Use it appropriately in the context of the situation, but be mindful of overfocussing on one side.
- Establish ground rules when working in a group.

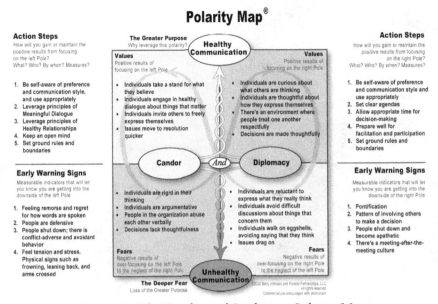

Figure 19: The Candor and Diplomacy Polarity Map

Implications for Polarity Intelligence

Leveraging candor and diplomacy is key to having dialogue around polarizing issues. It is also a key principle to follow when presenting your beliefs and perspectives so that others will hear you and respect your view.

How is Your Preference Pole Showing Up?

One of the things Tracy and I appreciate about long-term coaching with a team is seeing how their hard work pays off in growth. We've worked with one management team for several years. Part of our strategy includes measuring the core polarities they have been dealing with as a team and teaching them how to better leverage them. This particular team has worked hard on integrating meaningful dialogue—including how to apply the principles in their daily conversations.

As the team learned about the Candor and Diplomacy Polarity, they realized several things, including that while most of the managers preferred candor, they tended to act with diplomacy. They were able to appreciate the need for both Poles, and we challenged them to lean into their preference Pole more than they had in the past.

Once they mastered leveraging this polarity, they were able to achieve the Greater Purpose of healthy team communication. This, in turn, helped the entire management team to improve how they collaborated as a team and stay committed to their mutual goals and shared purpose.

Principle 5: Inviting Silence and Reflection

Talking is not the only way to engage in dialogue. Inviting or allowing for silence allows you to deepen your thinking and experience a connection with others. Silence requires you to be willing to reflect on lessons learned through words *not* spoken.

Many people are uncomfortable with silence. There can be a tendency to want to fill the void with words. At a typical work meeting, there are rarely moments of silence, let alone an invitation to reflect before speaking.

It's important that you allow time to sit in silence and reflect. This space allows us all to be fully present in listening—it opens the opportunity for us to practice Principal 2: Actively Listening and Being Aware.

Remember, when you actively listen, rather than formulating a response before someone else has even finished speaking, you gain understanding. When you pause for reflection, you can process what was said and respectfully consider the words and feelings being expressed.

Together, these principles enable you to tap into and add to the wisdom present.

Tips for Creating Dialogue by Inviting Silence and Reflection

- On your own, develop a practice of silence so you can be comfortable being silent with others.
- Be a role model of being comfortable with silence.
- Start a meeting or conversation with a moment of silence.
- Institute a reflection practice, an invitation for you and others to pause and collect their thoughts, then come back together for an opportunity to share insights with the group.

Implications for Polarity Intelligence

Silence in meaningful dialogue helps you to feel the connection between self and others. It allows you to reflect on your thoughts and reactions so you can learn from those and uncover tensions you are experiencing.

Reflecting on Self-Reflection

Tracy and I have noticed a pattern: Our clients seem to perceive little time for self-reflection. Yet, when we encourage them to pause and reflect, they welcome the opportunity to recenter. They value the time to get clear on their thoughts and desires. We hear them say things like:

"I can't remember the last time I did self-reflection."

"I didn't realize how lost I felt until I refocused on me."

"Thank you for the time to reflect."

Building dialogue skills calls for having a practice of quieting your mind and listening to yourself. Business icon Warren Buffett is known for taking significant, intentional time each day to just sit and think.[28] Not only does creativity call for time and space, so does effective self-dialogue. As a leader, it is imperative for you to become comfortable with silence with yourself first before you can invite silence into your time with others.

One way we suggest leaders do this is by establishing a morning ritual that includes a dedicated amount of time for silence and reflection. You may also find it helpful to schedule a few silent breaks throughout the day. Once you're comfortable with silence with yourself, you may also be more comfortable being silent in the presence of others.

Just like wisdom can spring from your personal time of silence, wisdom can spring from a time of collective silence, even in the middle of a group dialogue.

Silence and reflection can also be invited into other work settings. You can start meetings with a brief story, a meaningful statement, a thought-provoking question, or a poem, then follow it with a time of silence and reflection.

This intentional pause of silence helps to recenter people and transition them from whatever might be most on their minds (their to-do list, an upsetting email they just read, or what's next on their agenda) to the present moment.

When others are invited to share insights afterward, it can lead to a meaningful dialogue from which you can draw helpful insights.

At one of our gatherings, we asked leaders what their personal lessons have been on life's journeys. We then allowed a few minutes for silence before each leader shared their reflections. We followed this with a group dialogue on life's journeys and closed our gathering with a time of reflection again so partici-

---

28   https://bit.ly/BuffetThink

pants could give thought and consideration to their key learnings from the dialogue experience.

Some of the insights from the group dialogue were:

- "I was able to listen so much more when intentions were set prior to the dialogue."
- "Not thinking of a response helped me appreciate others' words."
- "Silence is hard."
- "I don't feel I have to fill the silence. (Getting better at this.)"
- "I realized my preference is diplomacy, and I need more courage with candor."

Taking time for silence and reflection enables us to better know ourselves as well as others.

Overview

As a leader, it's imperative that you master the skill of engaging in meaningful dialogue—a rich way of communicating and learning together. It is especially important during these polarizing times. Dialogue is an essential skill to creating a place of safety where you can explore polarities and engage others, using your different perspectives to serve a Greater Purpose. Below is a summary of each principle of meaningful dialogue.

- **Setting Intention and Creating Psychological Safety:** Starting with intention is the first step in creating a space for meaningful dialogue that is safe for sharing and for taking interpersonal risks.
- **Actively Listening and Being Aware:** Deep listening for learning from meaningful dialogue requires suspending assumptions and being aware of verbal and non-verbal communication, as well as emotions.

- **Balancing Advocacy and Inquiry:** Balancing advocacy and inquiry in meaningful dialogue requires awareness of when to use each—open sharing and asking questions—to uncover insights and new learning.
- **Leveraging Candor and Diplomacy:** Leveraging candor and diplomacy in meaningful dialogue welcomes speaking openly about beliefs and perceptions, while at the same time delivering a message with sensitivity and respect toward the recipients.
- **Inviting Silence and Reflection:** Wisdom and new learning are revealed in silence and reflection—a key principle to practice with yourself and with others. This creates space for listening and awareness.

Reflection Questions

1. When you know there is tension about an issue and you want to talk about it, what are ways you can share your intention before beginning the conversation?

2. Have you ever experienced talking to someone who stopped listening when you shared an opposing view? What was that like? What did you do to re-engage in dialogue? Have you done that to someone else?

3. When a topic with opposing views surfaces, do you lean more toward being candid in conversations, or are you more likely to be diplomatic?

4. In what ways do you incorporate silence into your life, especially when contemplating opposing views or values?

Call to Action

- Identify which meaningful dialogue principles you are strongest and weakest at using.

- Create a "practice field" with your team to practice meaningful dialogue.
- Start a meaningful dialogue journal. Set aside a regular quiet time for self-reflection. Begin by writing out the principles of meaningful dialogue. Then, use your journal to record your meaningful dialogue experiences and key learnings.
- Identify your preference Poles for the following polarities, then identify **one** action you can take to strengthen each Pole.
  - The Advocacy and Inquiry Polarity
  - The Candor and Diplomacy Polarity
  - Download a free PDF called **Practicing Meaningful Dialogue to Explore Polarities** from Polarityintelligence.com. Use this reference sheet to grow in Polarity Intelligence.

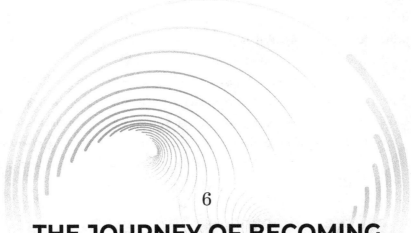

6

THE JOURNEY OF BECOMING
POLARITY INTELLIGENT

*Polarity Thinking in its simplicity is magical and in its
complexity is transformational. The integration of the principles of
relationships and dialogue with the principles of polarity
for continuous transformation of individuals and organizations
is the magnificent power of Polarity Intelligence.*
Bonnie Wesorick

By now, you know how to recognize polarities and how the principles of polarities help with your understanding of how they all work. You know that they all work the same way. You have been introduced to the principles of healthy relationships and the significance that relationships have in being polarity intelligent. And you grasp the principles of meaningful dialogue as an art and science of tapping the perspective and wisdom of others.

Now it's time to put it all together and cultivate Polarity Intelligence. When you integrate a **polarity mindset** with **healthy relationships** and add **meaningful dialogue** skills to the mix, you have a trifecta superpower.

But without *all three* of these and their principles *working together synergistically*, you will not experience the magnificent power of leading with Polarity Intelligence.

The Three Components of Polarity Intelligence

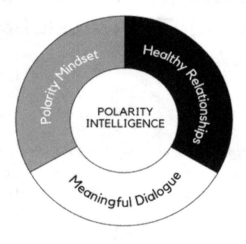

Figure 20: The Three Components of Polarity Intelligence

You can master one—even two—of the three components and still not be polarity intelligent. It is only when you have mastered *all three* that you will demonstrate the characteristics of a polarity intelligent leader. What follows are some scenarios that depict this reality. As you read through each of these scenarios, pause to reflect on how well you'd fare employing each of these skill sets in any given situation.

Polarity Mindset and Healthy Relationships
without Meaningful Dialogue

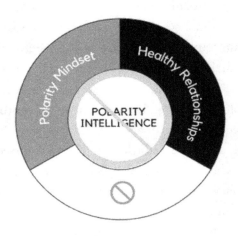

Figure 21: No Meaningful Dialogue? No Polarity Intelligence

There are leaders who understand the importance of thinking in terms of polarities and who have healthy relationships with their teams and family, yet they have never been exposed to the concept and principles of meaningful dialogue. Nor do they have the skill to use meaningful dialogue well in business or personal settings. As a result, they lack Polarity Intelligence. Why?

Meaningful dialogue helps you to skillfully explore and deepen your understanding of opposing views while maintaining or enhancing relationships. Without such dialogue, it is difficult to explore both Poles of a polarity. And without understanding both Poles, it is hard to transcend personal biases and achieve a Greater Purpose.

- Without meaningful dialogue, you can have healthy relationships with others—and even be aware of polarities and committed to a shared purpose—yet still be unable to uncover differing perspectives. As a result, you won't be able to adequately understand and name the polarities being experienced, nor will you be able to gain insights and wisdom from the opposing views or values.

- Without a safe space to share perspectives, deepen insights, and gain truthful information—all fostered through meaningful dialogue—others will hold back and not speak their truth. If they feel at risk interpersonally, they will not feel psychologically safe. This can impact how others respond to your request for feedback. It affects Polarity Assessment data as well. Accurate information will get missed if others are not candid with their perspectives. The lack of candor and diplomacy also masks reality and prevents progress toward desired outcomes.

- You may be aware of the value of healthy relationships and the significance of polarities; however, it is the meaningful dialogue that helps you leverage and manage the tensions collectively with another person or a group. You could be aware of a polarity that exists and the fact that your team is dealing with one, yet it is in using meaningful dialogue skills that you tap the collective wisdom and deepen understanding of its context, overcome biases, and discover the best way to leverage the polarity collectively.

- Without meaningful dialogue, you also limit the deepening of your relationships and the creating of shared understanding of how polarities are working *with* you and *on* you. These realities can only be adequately explored via meaningful dialogue.

- A lack of meaningful dialogue can frustrate you as a leader. You care about your people and are aware of the polarity at hand, but it is by using meaningful dialogue that you access the confidence to engage others in conversation about polarities.

Case Study: Holly's Lightbulb Moments

Holly is a leader at a large US university and has been leading regional and national educational competency work for over twenty years. Highly regarded as a scholar in her field, she is well known in her industry and has a large network of professional relationships.

Holly was also a master at creating strong relationships with professional and state organizations and getting them engaged on large-scale implementation and research projects. Her passion and desire to make a difference for her profession was palpable.

One of the large-scale studies revealed significant unintended consequences related to new technology being rapidly implemented across multiple facilities.

Holly consulted with us at MissingLogic, and we and did a deep dive on polarities. This helped her make sense of a unipolar focus revealed in their study. Holly had a lightbulb moment as she connected the dots on how important it is to understand polarities in order to create sustainable change. She commited to grow her polarity mindset.

Back at the office, Holly shared what she had learned with several others in her network. It didn't take long before she became very frustrated, though. She felt inept at engaging others in conversations when she recognized what was being experienced was a polarity and not a problem.

"I find myself getting anxious," Holly told us. "I want to bring the polarity out into the open and explore together the tension we are feeling. I want to get to the bottom of a recurring issue, but I'm not sure where to start. And sometimes I get so worked up because of my Pole preference that I'm afraid I am going to blow it ... so I don't go there."

The truth is that despite being a successful leader and scholar in her field, Holly had never been introduced to meaningful dialogue as a *skill*. She experienced what many other leaders do: being in meetings where people talk over each other, people holding on to their biases, speaking either too much or not enough about what they really think, and rarely having time for silence and reflection.

Learning about the principles of meaningful dialogue was another lightbulb moment for Holly. She grasped how critical this skill was for identifying and exploring polarities. Knowing that meaningful dialogue would create a shared understanding and a common language to an experience not only increased Holly's confidence as a leader, but it also enhanced her Polarity Intelligence.

One of the tools we had Holly use to strengthen her dialogue skills was the **Meaningful Dialogue Introspection Tool and Worksheet.** It is available to download at Polarityintelligence.com. Using this tool in real-time conversations gave Holly the confidence to practice her dialogue skills. Now, she's able to uncover and explore polarities with her colleagues.

Meaningful Dialogue and Healthy Relationships
without a Polarity Mindset

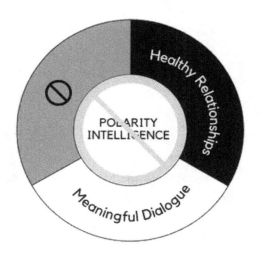

Figure 22: No Polarity Mindset? No Polarity Intelligence

There are leaders who have excellent communication and relationship skills; however, they've never heard about Polarity Thinking, nor do they understand what polarities are and how they impact them and their team every day.

Without a *polarity* mindset, leaders only live and lead from a *problem* mindset. This leads to predictable Negative Outcomes. Changes made may have Positive Outcomes at first, but over time if only one Pole in a polarity is addressed and there are not Action Steps followed on the *other* Pole of the polarity, it is 100% guaranteed that the Negative Outcomes will show up.

- When you lack a polarity mindset, you engage others to work collectively on solving problems. You are engaging in meaningful conversations; however, without being able to differentiate a problem from a polarity, you repeatedly experience the same issues. You may see success initially, but this success is not sustainable if the problem is indeed a polarity.

- It's difficult to sustain a shared purpose if there is no clarity on the chronic tensions that exist and how they are impacting you, your relationships, and your environment. This is true even within healthy relationships.

- The lack of polarity awareness means polarities aren't identified, measured, or leveraged. This puts you and your organization at risk of unintended consequences.

- Healthy relationships can become strained over time if polarities such as Productivity and Relationships, Process and Progress, and Individual and Team aren't leveraged.

- Meaningful dialogue can reveal new insights into an issue you may be dealing with, but if you don't recognize any interdependent pairs at play, you will still only see an incomplete picture of the situation. This leaves wisdom on the table, which can lead to either wrong actions or not enough action being taken.

Case Study: Justin's Dilemma of Choosing between Options

Justin is the CEO of an online learning platform for young adult learners. The company had goals for scaling internationally, and Justin was finding that his leadership team was having opposing perspectives on how to get there.

Some thought the company should allocate some resources to increase their marketing efforts so young adults could know the company exists. Others thought they should continue to upgrade their platform and courses so customers would have an exceptional experience. They believed that this, in turn, might drive sales.

Justin himself was torn on how to solve this dilemma. Should they increase marketing spend and outreach, or should they make the best online learning platform and a quality product?

One thing he knew was that the tension was mounting. Meanwhile, time and money were being wasted as folks on different sides of the issue panicked. They insisted on pausing and revisiting the issue.

Justin knew he could figure this problem out; surely things would improve if he used his relationship skills and doubled down on his communication efforts. Justin and his team had some great dialogue skills they had learned in an executive training program, so he reminded them that if they engaged in meaningful dialogue some innovation would emerge. This helped at times, but after a while Justin noticed a pattern—they kept coming back to the same points.

Justin took healthy relationships very seriously and invested intentional time connecting one-on-one with his leadership team. He reminded them that they all had equal responsibility for the mission and growth of the company.

Despite Justin's superb relational skills, his leadership team found themselves in a stalemate—they couldn't agree on the best strategy to scale internationally.

Justin was sharing about this "problem" in his business mastermind. One of his cohort members—someone who had learned about the polarity mindset from his marketing coach and knew enough to recognize Justin's dilemma was a polarity—asked him, "Justin, is this a problem to solve, or could it be a polarity to leverage?"

Having never heard of the term *polarity*, Justin asked the mastermind colleague to explain more. The colleague grabbed a piece of paper and made a back-of-a-napkin map, right there on the spot.

Justin's colleague drew one line down and another one across the middle. On the left he wrote "Marketing/Outreach," and on the right he wrote "Platform/Product."

After a quick walk through the Positive Outcomes of both Poles and why they were both needed to achieve the Greater Purpose of scaling the business internationally, it was clear to Justin what his team needed. They needed to stop competing for *either* marketing *or* platform funding. They needed both. If they could put some action into *both* strategies, their Greater Purpose would be achieved.

Justin left the mastermind meeting with a new sense of hope for how he and his team could dynamically balance this polarity. He couldn't wait to get home and call a leadership council meeting and have them look at this challenge through a polarity lens.

Over time Justin became a polarity intelligent leader and used the **Polarity Introspection Tool and Worksheet** to help identify polarities in his real-life experiences both at work and at home. That tool is available to download at Polarityintelligence.com.

Polarity Mindset and Meaningful Dialogue *without Healthy Relationships*

There are leaders who have a polarity mindset and can engage in meaningful dialogue, yet they have not prioritized building healthy relationships with themselves and their teams. Without that component, they lack Polarity Intelligence.

When everyone is talking at meetings, it can be easy to assume that everyone is getting along and that your team is connecting and collaborating. And when you assume everything is fine, you don't bother putting in effort—including training and other infrastructures, like councils—to support relationship building.

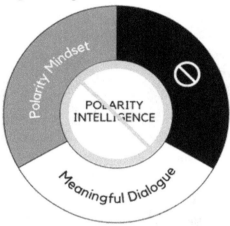

Figure 23: No Healthy Relationships? No Polarity Intelligence

- Without having healthy relationships, you might understand polarities and could be having conversation about them; however, there is a lack of shared purpose and equal responsibility to leverage the polarity. This results in a lack of commitment and action on the part of your team.

- Without a focus on having a healthy relationship with others, you can overfocus on *your* needs and be perceived as not being a good partner.

- You can also miss out on opportunities to recognize and grow others in the skills of gaining a polarity mindset and engaging in meaningful dialogue.

- Without a focus on having healthy relationships, the relationships at home and at the office will become transactional, which makes it more difficult to engage others in dialogue and explore polarities together.

Case Study: Kelly's Roadblock to Success

Kelly is a senior manager at a global information technology company. She is passionate about her development as a leader and has taken it upon herself to advance her management skills with every learning opportunity she can get.

Through her company, Kelly took management classes and attended conferences to enhance her leadership skills. Kelly attended a polarity workshop that we facilitated. As Kelly developed a polarity mindset, she recognized common polarities she and her team would need to leverage:

- Technology Alignment and Business Alignment
- Short-Term Solutions and Long-Term Solutions
- Information Security and Information Flow

During our workshop, Kelly practiced how to begin a dialogue with others by setting intention and creating psychological safety. She used dialogue skills to listen for polarities to ask genuine questions to uncover preference Poles and biases. While still a novice, she was thrilled how the dialogue skills were already helping her manage situations at work and at home.

Back at the office, Kelly engaged her team in conversation on how to best leverage the common polarities identified for their department. Then she shared the insights with her director.

Over time, one of the patterns that Kelly began to recognize was that she felt alone in the process. In fact, she sensed resentment from her team for applying this new way of thinking and for asking every week how their Action Steps were going. Staff engagement even started dropping in Kelly's department, and Kelly's director expressed concern about it.

Kelly knew she had communicated her learnings and expectations for getting things done very well, so she wondered what was going wrong.

One thing Kelly had neglected to do was to use the principles of healthy relationships to establish a good partnership with her director and her team. Through our coaching, Kelly recognized that while her expectations were clear, she was not clear on what others' expectations were of her. And while she had been good at communicating broadly, she had missed the opportunity to be more intentional regarding connecting with others and recognizing the human capacity of each team member.

Kelly was emotional when sharing, "Of course I value relationships. It was hard to realize that I wasn't being very intentional in my presence with my team members. I also recognized that I tend to focus more on my goals to the neglect of what their growth and development goals are. Ouch! In the end, I guess you could say I haven't been managing the Task and Relationship Polarity very well!"

We all chuckled at this insight, and Tracy and I pointed out that this was a great key learning—awareness is the first step in adding this component and growing her Polarity Intelligence.

One of the tools we had Kelly use with her director and team members was the **Healthy Relationship/Partnership Agreement Tool**. It is available to download at Polarityintelligence.com.

* * *

As a reminder, you cultivate Polarity Intelligence by integrating a polarity mindset with healthy relationships and meaningful dialogue skills. When these components and their principles—summarized in Table 3—work together synergistically, you will experience the power of leading with Polarity Intelligence.

Table 3. A Compilation of the Principles of Polarity Intelligence

Polarity Mindset
1. **Knowing the purpose of interdependent values or points of view (polarities)** • Both Poles are equally important • Alone, neither Pole can reach the Greater Purpose • Tension is good and can be leveraged
2. **Recognizing there is always invisible energy flowing between and around the interdependent pair** • When the Positive Outcomes of both Poles are achieved, the energy is positive and flows toward the Greater Purpose • When you overemphasize one Pole or overfocus on one and neglect the other, you experience Negative Outcomes of the Pole you focused on
3. **Preventing unintended consequences is possible** • The negative consequences of overfocusing on one Pole is a loss of the Positive Outcomes of the opposite Pole • To avoid the Deeper Fear, you must simultaneously pay attention to both Poles so you can achieve the Positive Outcomes of each
4. **Leveraging polarities creates sustainable desired outcomes** • The only way to leverage a polarity is to implement the Action Steps simultaneously • The objective of leveraging a polarity is to achieve a state of dynamic balance • When focus is heavily weighted on one Pole, you must place enough focus on the oppositive Pole to maintain the Positive Outcomes of that Pole

Healthy Relationships
1. **Being intentional** • A conscious choice to be 100% present and connect at the inner-being or soul level of another person
2. **Establishing a shared purpose** • The relationship centers around coming together for a common goal
3. **Recognizing equal responsibility** • A relationship driven by accepting mutual responsibility in achieving the shared purpose
4. **Realizing human capacity** • The potential in oneself and others to continually learn, grow and become
5. **Balancing relationship with self and other** • The dynamic balance between self and other(s) to achieve a shared purpose

6. **Being trustworthy**
   - Knowing personal trustworthiness precedes a trusting relationship with one another

Meaningful Dialogue

1. **Setting intention and creating psychological safety**
   - The clarity of your intention and then sharing your intention with others is the first step in creating a safe container for dialogue
   - The willingness to create a safe place, to be clear on what you desire from the heart, and to be influenced making it possible to achieve shared understanding
   - Welcoming the voice of others in an open and authentic way creating an environment that is safe for interpersonal risk-taking
2. **Actively listening and being aware**
   - The willingness to learn by intense listening to self and others, not to analyze, prove, compete, judge, rescue, fix, or blame
   - Suspending assumptions while listening to others
   - Being aware of all verbal and non-verbal communication and emotions
3. **Balancing advocacy and inquiry**
   - The willingness to share non-scripting thinking and what is behind that thinking, with the intention of exposing, not defending it
   - The willingness to ask genuine questions that dig deeper and uncover insights and new learning
   - Being aware of your personal preference toward advocacy and inquiry to help balance the two during conversation
4. **Leveraging candor and diplomacy**
   - The willingness to speak openly and frankly, with honest beliefs or perceptions, *and to* speak with sensitivity toward the recipient(s) of the message
   - Recognizing both are important for meaningful conversation and achieving a shared understanding
5. **Inviting silence and reflection**
   - The willingness to reflect on lessons learned from personal awareness or words unspoken
   - Recognizing the power of both self and group reflection to reveal wisdom and new learning

You can download a copy of this summary from Polarityintelligence.com. It is also in the Addendum.

Becoming polarity intelligent as a leader takes awareness and practice. One way to build your Polarity Intelligence is to use the **Polarity Intelligence Intention and Reflection Worksheet** that pulls all three components together. You can download it from Polarityintelligence.com. You can use this worksheet daily, or when you want to show up with your Polarity Intelligence superpower in full force.

Next, we'll look at how you can measure the polarities you experience in your professional and personal life.

Overview

- Polarity Intelligence has three main components: polarity mindset, healthy relationships, and meaningful dialogue. Each component is grounded in principles, and when you apply those synergistically, you exhibit Polarity Intelligence. If one of the three components isn't present, then Polarity Intelligence does not fully exist.

- The case studies each demonstrate how the outcome is affected if one of the three components is missing from the Polarity Intelligence equation. Each case study includes a helpful reflection tool you can download and use to build awareness and strengthen the missing component.

Reflection Questions

1. Use the Likert scale below to estimate how well you apply the principles from all three components in your life.
2. Which component is your strongest?
3. In which area do you see your greatest need for growth in order to expand your Polarity Intelligence?
4. How might you begin to cultivate Polarity Intelligence on your team?

Call to Action

- Download the principles of each Polarity Intelligence component and review them. Circle the principles you would like to intentionally focus on to enhance your Polarity Intelligence as a leader. Revisit the list weekly to check your progress.
- Download the free resources at Polarityintelligence.com and apply them in your leadership role.
- Put together a plan to cultivate a polarity intelligent team.

Polarity Mindset

I rarely use it   I sometimes use it   I often use it

Healthy Relationships

I am terrible at this   I am growing in this   I am great at this

Meaningful Dialogue

I rarely use it   I sometimes use it   I often use it

7

MONITORING AND MEASURING
THE LEVERAGING OF POLARITIES

All improvements begin by reconnecting with the ideal.
Michael Hyatt

Now what? How do you apply what you have learned so you know
how you're experiencing personal or organizational polarities? In
this chapter, you'll learn how to monitor your individual progress when leveraging personal polarities. We'll also introduce you to an
assessment tool we use in our consulting and coaching programs to measure the experience of many stakeholders when leveraging organizational
polarities. This tool gives you a real-time measurement of reality. It also
helps you to measure the sustainability of the outcomes over time.

Real-time measurements can indicate Positive Outcomes, but without measurement *over time*, you cannot determine if the Action Steps you've taken have been effective and whether the outcomes are sustainable. When you know the Action Steps are working or not, you can make course corrections and avoid unintended negative consequences.

We'll also expand more on how you can achieve dynamic balance by leveraging the energy between the Poles in a polarity. This requires that you vigilantly monitor for Early Warning Signs so you can make course corrections as needed. Only when you achieve the dynamic balance of seeing sustainable Positive Outcomes of both Poles will it lead to the Greater Purpose you're after.

Monitoring the Leveraging of Personal Polarities

As noted in previous chapters, polarities are everywhere. As a leader, you face both personal and organizational polarities. To get to the Greater Purpose of a polarity, it's not enough to know that polarities exist.

You can create a Polarity Map for any polarity you are experiencing to make the polarity more concrete and visible. Creating the map is the first step. You must use the map to guide your behaviors if you want to achieve the Greater Purpose.

As you may recall from Chapter 3, the only polarity that is leveraged *for us* is inhaling and exhaling. To leverage any other polarity, you must intentionally take simultaneous Action Steps in order to achieve the Positive Outcomes of *both* Poles and vigilantly monitor for Early Warning Signs so that you can course correct when necessary to avoid the Negative Outcomes.

The simplest way to monitor your progress in leveraging personal polarities is to look at your polarity map frequently (once a week to once a month) and assess if you are experiencing any Early Warning Signs. Next evaluate how frequently you are experiencing each of the Positive Outcomes and Negative Consequences you have identified.

Your results will inform which actions to take. As an example, if you are experiencing Early Warning Signs that is an indicator you may be over focusing on one Pole and neglecting the other or the Action Step you identified may not be as effective as you thought it would be. In either instance, it's time to re-evaluate the Action Steps you identified to achieve the Positive Outcome and possibly increase the frequency with which you apply the Action Step or modify or replace the Action Step. We've created a free resource for monitoring how well you are leveraging your personal polarities that you can download at Polarityintelligence.com.

The Polarity Assessment™ Instrument

In Chapter 2, we identified how important it is for you as a leader to have a complete and accurate picture of current reality. This is also true when it comes to the stakeholders' experience of a polarity. Without assessing what all stakeholders are experiencing, it is difficult to identify the necessary Action Steps and evaluate their effectiveness.

Under the leadership of Barry Johnson, the team at Polarity Partnerships developed an instrument to measure, in real time, the degree to which one or more polarities are leveraged. Johnson calls this a Polarity Assessment.

This assessment makes the experience of the polarity more tangible. It also helps you and other stakeholders see the degree of success you are having leveraging the polarity. This, in turn, allows you and the stakeholders to evaluate specific Action Steps to determine which steps are either supporting or inhibiting the Positive Outcomes you're striving for.

The Polarity Assessment is web-based, making it easy to distribute and reach all stakeholders—as long as they have access to the internet. What's more, participants don't have to have any knowledge of polarities to complete the assessment because the instrument is simply asking the respondent to rate the degree to which they are experiencing the Positive or Negative Outcomes of each Pole using a Likert-type scale.

The assessment also has filtering capabilities, allowing you to gain insight on the perspectives of individuals in specific roles, teams, or groups.

Characteristics of the Polarity Assessment

1. It Measures Interdependence

Historically, your company may have used outcome metrics and key performance indicators to validate the effectiveness of real-time problem-solving. But since problem-solving involves either/or thinking, measurements based on the problem-solving logic gauge outcomes without considering the impact of the interdependencies between deeply held values. Metrics and KPIs also do not look at the sustainability of the outcome over time.

This is one of the reasons why the same problems show up again and again. When you use a problem-solving approach to address a polarity, there is a lack of awareness of the interdependent Poles. Likewise, you may be blissfully unaware of the need for simultaneous action so you can achieve Positive Outcomes for *both* Poles.

Since problem-solving involves either/or thinking, measurements based on the problem-solving logic gauge outcomes without considering the impact of the interdependencies between deeply held values. Metrics and KPIs also do not gauge the sustainability of the outcome over time.

Also, as we shared in Chapter 2, polarities exist at the individual, leadership, organizational, community, and national levels. Since they *exist* at all those levels, they must be *measured* at each level—something you cannot do with metrics and KPIs.

Think about it. Leadership performance assessments measure the presence of key leadership characteristics along a continuum. These assessments typically have a desired characteristic on one end of the continuum and the related undesired characteristic on the other end. The focus of such assessments is to determine to what degree the desired characteristic is present or not. In other words, these assessments are built on an either/or approach without considering any possible interdependencies.

Using this approach can lead to false assumptions about a leader's strengths and weaknesses. And such false assumptions ultimately lead to ineffective strategies for supporting the growth and development of leaders.

Let's say, for example, Jane and John are managers at a food produce company that is set on creating a thriving work environment.

Jane values her role in supporting her team to be as productive as possible. Her team has been successful at completing several initiatives on time—some even ahead of schedule. John, meanwhile, values developing healthy relationships with his team. As a result, John's team is highly engaged, though they don't always meet their goals.

If we were to measure Jane and John's effectiveness as leaders based on productivity, Jane would rank high in her ability to keep the team focused and productive. Using the same measure, John might rank lower since productivity is not his focus.

However, if we were to look at effectiveness through the lens of relationships between leaders and their teams, John would rank high due to his ability to establish healthy relationships with his team while Jane may rank low because this is not where she is putting most of her efforts.

The assessment results may be an accurate snapshot of a specific leadership characteristic, but when you don't know about polarities it leads to an incomplete picture, and an incomplete picture will lead to false assumptions about the effectiveness of Jane and John's leadership.

But when you use a polarity mindset and apply a Polarity Assessment to measure effective leadership, the interdependency between Productivity and Relationships is clear, as is the need for both to be present to achieve a thriving work environment. It also becomes evident one is not more important than the other.

Work environments are complex and constantly evolving. This requires different levels of expression of both Poles at different times. It also requires leaders to be flexible in how they use these skills and maintain dynamic balance between them.

This is why monitoring the polarity over time is essential.

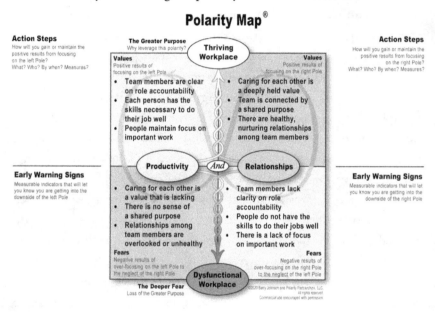

Figure 24: Productivity and Relationship Polarity Map

An assessment of this interdependent relationship provides you with a more complete picture of the potential effectiveness of both Jane and John. It also enables them to establish and prioritize actions that will help them see the need to attend to the Pole that they naturally neglect. It also allows them and their management to monitor for opportunities to make course corrections over time.

2. It Can Be Both Customizable and Standardized

By now, you know that you can customize every Polarity Map so that it represents the unique experience, knowledge, and priorities of your organization. And since the assessment is based on your maps, the outcomes of the Polarity Assessment represent your unique experience.

Since many organizations and teams face the same polarities, though, the assessment also allows you to use standardized content to examine your outcomes—whether positive or negative—and create benchmark data across multiple organizations or internal teams that are attempting to leverage the same polarities.

The work done by Bonnie Wesorick is an excellent example of such a standardized approach. She created a standardized Polarity Assessment called the CPM (Clinical Practice Model) Polarity Assessment for Healthcare (CPAH). Wesorick used this to measure thirteen common polarities (see Table 4) faced by member organizations in the CPM Consortium. In partnership with Dr. Steve Shaha, she studied four healthcare organizations in the healthcare consortium to examine the stakeholders' experience of each polarity and determine the reliability of the CPAH instrument.[29]

This valid and reliable instrument gave leaders in the CPM consortium a standardized approach to measuring the thirteen common polarities that all the organizations faced and had historically been treated as problems. The diagnostic information enabled them to identify and prioritize actions steps that would support the achievement of the greater purpose and sustainable success.

Imagine what having a standardized Polarity Assessment could do for you in helping you assess and leverage polarities that are experienced all across your organization.

---

29 Wesorick, B. and Shaha, S., "Guiding Healthcare Transformation: A Next-Generation Diagnostic Remediation Tool for Leveraging Polarities," *Nursing Outlook*. Nov.–Dec. 2015

Table 4. CPM Polarity Assessment for Healthcare Polarities

CPAH Polarities
Patient Safety and Staff Safety
Routine Task Care and Scope of Practice Care
Individual Competency and Team Competency
Standardized Care and Autonomous Care
Conditional Respect and Unconditional Respect
Vertical Relationships and Horizontal Relationships
Medical Care and Whole-Person Care
Technology Platform and Practice Platform
Patient Satisfaction and Staff Satisfaction
Candor and Diplomacy
Change and Stability
Project/Initiative-Driven Change and Framework-Driven Change
Margin and Mission

3. It Produces Real-Time Results

Rather than painting a picture of a day sometime in the past, online assessment results are available in real time. This gives you invaluable information regarding current perceptions. And when you document those results, you also have a way to measure the effectiveness of strategies as you go.

These measurements show how well the polarity is being leveraged. It also lets you see how often stakeholders experience each Positive and Negative Outcome. Analysis of the results can reveal how effective your strategies are at supporting the achievement of the desired outcomes. It can also reveal which conditions may either be inhibiting or supporting you reaching your desired outcomes and Greater Purpose.

4. It Is Scalable

You can use a web-based Polarity Assessment to assess polarities at the individual, team, organizational, community, and even at a national level. Here are four examples of how organizations and teams in the United States are utilizing these assessments.

5. Individual Polarity Assessment

In our work to assist healthcare leaders in becoming thriving, resilient, and unstoppable (TRU) leaders, we developed the Dynamic Balance Assessment.™ This standardized assessment includes four personal polarities that leaders have to leverage to succeed as TRU leaders. These are Professional and Personal Life, Caring for Self and Caring for Others, Activity and Rest, and Productivity and Relationships.

We ask individuals to complete a self-assessment. We also ask them to have close friends, family, and colleagues complete the assessment. This allows us to get a multi-perspective view of how well these leaders are leveraging the four polarities. The results inevitably show differences between the self-assessment and the perspective of others close to them.

After receiving their results, individuals identify Action Steps and Early Warning Signs for all the polarities. Such an individual assessment helps leaders focus their attention and behaviors and take ownership of their Polarity Intelligence growth.

6. Team Polarity Assessment

It's not uncommon for us to find teams struggling with recurring challenges. We recently worked with a leadership team in this situation. We started by dialoguing with many of the team members to uncover four core polarities that were influencing their effectiveness in working collectively as a leadership team—Candor and Diplomacy, Competition and Collaboration, Structure and Flexibility, and Task and Relationship. Then, we developed a Polarity Assessment and distributed it to all the team members.

We used the initial assessment to gather a baseline measurement of the leaders' real-time experience of the polarities individually as well as collectively. Next, we facilitated a leadership team retreat where we taught them about Polarity Intelligence, helped them explore the four polarities, and increased their awareness of the importance of establishing healthy relationships and engaging in meaningful dialogue as a team.

Notice we didn't start by teaching the team how to be polarity intelligent. We assessed how well they were leveraging the polarities impacting the team. Next, we used the results as the impetus to embrace a new paradigm of Polarity Intelligence. In the same way, you don't have to train your team in Polarity Intelligence before you can assess how they are leveraging a polarity or polarities.

Collectively, these leaders identified Action Steps and Early Warning Signs for each of the four polarities.

A year later, we conducted a repeat assessment. The results from the second assessment showed that the team had used Polarity Intelligence to successfully leverage all four polarities.

7. Organizational Polarity Assessment

The College of Allied Health Sciences (CAHS) at the University of Cincinnati embraced a polarity mindset when they created their strategic plan in 2015. One of their goals was "Fostering a culture of inclusion … to attract a diverse student body, faculty, and staff…"[30]

They developed an assessment to measure how CAHS was leveraging the Recruiting Diversity and Retaining Diversity Polarity. The leadership team distributed the Polarity Assessment to faculty and staff at the college, including multiple departments and levels of leadership.

The results indicated that the faculty and staff often experienced the Positive Outcomes associated with both Poles, indicating they were leveraging this polarity well at the time the assessment was done.

8. International Polarity Assessment

The Center for Creative Leadership (CCL) conducted a study on creating and sustaining virtual teamwork effectiveness on an international scale[31]. Their research explored the role certain polarities play in the effectiveness of virtual teams. Participants in the study included 140 virtual teams from a diverse range of industries and countries.

At the start of the study, the CCL distributed assessments to the virtual teams. Six months later, they sent out a follow-up assessment. This allowed them to notice changes in the polarities over time and the impact these had on team effectiveness.

They measured eight polarities:

- Advocacy and Inquiry
- Formal Communication and Informal Communication
- Verify and Trust
- Physically Apart and Physically Together
- Flexible Schedule and Traditional Schedule

---

30 Labiner, G., Hobek, A., and Wilkins, M. "From Vision to Execution: One College's Commitment to Diversity, Equity, and Inclusion." National Academies of Practice, 2022 Annual Meeting and Forum, March 3–5, 2022, San Diego, CA.

31 Center for Creative Leadership. "Creating and Sustaining Virtual Team Effectiveness." *2017 Final Research Report.*

- Unified Team and Diverse Individuals
- Task Focused and Relationship Orientation
- Creating New Processes and Using Existing Processes

The results indicated that in the areas where the polarities were leveraged well, CCL's international virtual teams were experiencing effective teamwork.

From this study, it is clear that you can evaluate multiple polarities through a single Polarity Assessment, then reevaluate them after some time. What's more, it shows that large numbers of stakeholders from multiple locations can participate in the assessment.

9. It Supports Dynamic Balance

In Chapter 3, we listed the principles of polarities. Principle 8 stated, "When focus is heavily weighted on one Pole, you must place enough focus on the opposite Pole to at least maintain the Positive Outcomes of that Pole."

In other words, you leverage a polarity to achieve a state of dynamic balance.

Dynamic balance is like walking a tightrope—you must keep your attention on the Greater Purpose you are striving to get to. As you move toward that Greater Purpose, you must make small but impactful adjustments based on Early Warning Signs to maintain your balance. If you overcompensate one way or the other, you'll fall into unintentional negative consequences.

As a leader, if you're not vigilant in monitoring for the Early Warning Sings and measuring the current status of your core organizational polarities, you may easily overemphasize one Pole to the neglect of the other. You also might tolerate Action Steps that are ineffective.

The VUCA nature of today's environment requires that you choose Action Steps that enable you to be flexible. In being flexible, you are more likely to find the dynamic balance you need to leverage the polarity for your Greater Purpose. Along with that, you need to nurture healthy relationships and meaningful dialogue so you can quickly evaluate the present-day realities and make rapid course corrections.

Using a Polarity Assessment is the best way to determine whether your strategies are effective in maintaining this dynamic balance and Virtuous Cycle toward your Greater Purpose. But for Early Warning Signs to be effective in helping you recognize impending negative consequences, ineffective strategies, or a unipolar emphasis, you need leaders who are polarity intelligent.

Now it's time to put it all together and see what life looks like when you have greater Polarity Intelligence.

Overview

- Being able to identify a polarity and engaging with others through healthy relationships and dialogue isn't enough to be considered polarity intelligent.
- The best way to leverage an organizational polarity is to examine how stakeholders are experiencing the polarity. You do so by measuring present-day realities of those stakeholders, evaluating the effectiveness of current strategies, and making adjustments to Action Steps based on Early Warning Signs so that you can avoid unintended negative consequences.
- You can reach a Dynamic Balance through vigilant monitoring, making course corrections, and leveraging of the energy between the Poles to achieve the Greater Purpose and sustainable Positive Outcomes.

Reflection Questions

1. Where in your life, personally or professionally, are you attempting to improve your situation without measuring your current realities or the outcomes of your Action Steps?

2. In what ways have you benefited in the past, as an individual or as a leader, from outcome measurements or assessments?

3. Where, personally or organizationally, are you currently measuring outcomes or performance from an either/or, unipolar, or problem-solving approach?

Call to Action

• Identify how you, your team, and your organization could benefit from identifying and then assessing polarities.

• Deepen your understanding of the Polarity Assessment at Polarityintelligence.com.

8

THE CALL FOR POLARITY INTELLIGENCE IN LEADERSHIP

*Take a deep breath and say, "Hey, both of these can be true."
And that energy that we create holding opposite things (tension)
is the birthplace of transformation. The ability to straddle
paradoxes really leads to transformation. Not only are tensions
OK and normal—they're the magic sauce.*
Brené Brown

Having the understanding of Polarity Intelligence that you now have, can you see why it's a crucial skill all leaders should grow in? Imagine how different the world would be if Polarity Intelligence were to become a leadership norm and a common competency for leaders in all industries.

Leaders with a high Polarity Intelligence are masters at creating and leveraging healthy relationships and meaningful dialogue. Doing so, they engage others to transcend beyond diverse perspectives and experiences, creating thriving work cultures despite the nature of the times we live in.

In Chapter 1, we mentioned that the world we live in calls for new forms of operations and new ways of thinking. More than ever, the world needs leaders with a high Polarity Intelligence to lead through these volatile, uncertain, complex, and ambiguous (VUCA) situations.

A leader who is polarity intelligent can identify the interdependencies inherent in these situations—seeing connections that might not be obvious to others—and leverage the polarity to achieve a Greater Purpose with sustainable Positive Outcomes.

There are many polarities inherent to the VUCA nature of our times. Here are some examples.

Table 5. Polarities Inherent to a VUCA World

VUCA Elements	Examples of Inherent Polarities
Volatile	Change and Stability Flexibility and Structure
Uncertain	Caution and Boldness Risk-Taking and Protecting
Complex	Independence and Connectedness Interdependence and Self-Reliance
Ambiguous	Reflection and Action Directive Decision-Making and Shared Decision-Making

Leaders who are committed to raising their Polarity Intelligence open their mind to continuous and adaptive learning. They practice seeking the shared purpose at the heart of healthy relationships while honoring the differences. They do so through meaningful dialogue.

So, how do you increase your Polarity Intelligence? You work at becoming unconsciously competent at applying Polarity Intelligence.

Becoming Unconsciously Competent at Polarity Intelligence

In the early 1970s, Noel Burch from Gordon Training International—a company focusing on relational effectiveness—described a four-step process for learning any new skill.[32] Nowadays, it's referred to as the four stages of competence:

1. Unconscious incompetence (ignorance of lack of skill)
2. Conscious incompetence (awareness of lack of skill)
3. Conscious competence (learning)
4. Unconscious competence (mastery)

Table 6 shows what this looks like as we grow in Polarity Intelligence.

---

32 Gordon Training International, "Learning a New Skill is Easier Said Than Done." https://bit.ly/3P330IO

Table 6. Polarity Intelligence and the Four Stages of Competence

Unconscious Incompetence	Conscious Incompetence	Conscious Competence	Unconscious Competence
You don't know what you don't know	You are aware of the knowledge gap	You know about Polarity Intelligence but it's not easy to apply	You use Polarity Intelligence without having to think about it
• Not knowing anything about Polarity Intelligence, it is unlikely that you will engage in a sustainable solution • You might realize there's tension, but you don't know that those tensions are polarities • You're unaware of the impact of imbalanced polarities on yourself and on others	• You know that polarities exist but not how to manage them • You require validation of polarities you suspect are at play • You desire to learn from others with greater competence in Polarity Intelligence	• You know how to differentiate between a polarity and a problem • You're learning to create a Polarity Map and can manage polarities • Rather than needing more training, you may simply need time to practice applying the components of Polarity Intelligence • You reflect on what you are learning by applying Polarity Intelligence	• You can leverage polarities as effectively as you can solve problems • You naturally engage others in the process of leveraging polarities • You ask questions no one else asks

Looking at the descriptions of Polarity Intelligence along the stages of competence, did you notice the final characteristic of leaders who are at the mastery level? Why is it that once you're at a level of unconscious competence, you'll ask different questions? It's because the questions flow from the principles of polarities, healthy relationships, and meaningful dialogue.

When you are unconsciously competent at applying Polarity Intelligence, you are fully present with others. You ask the questions that intentionally bring out a perspective that others wouldn't think of asking.

Why is it that once you're at a level of unconscious competence, you'll ask different questions? It's because the questions flow from the principles of polarities, healthy relationships, and meaningful dialogue.

* * *

Barry Johnson—the organizational development expert who teaches Polarity Thinking and who designed the Polarity Assessment—wrote two volumes on Polarity Intelligence called *And: Making a Difference by Leveraging Polarity, Paradox or Dilemma*. In the first volume, *Foundations*, Johnson describes a five-step process for getting unstuck from either/or thinking.[33]

Using Johnson's process, Table 7 shows how the Healthy Relationship Principles and Meaningful Dialogue Principles apply to each step of helping someone—including yourself—get unstuck.

---

33 Johnson, B. 2020. *And: Making a Difference by Leveraging Polarity, Paradox and Dilemma. Volume One: Foundations.* Amherst MA. HRD Press. p.105.

Table 7. The Five-Step Process of Getting Unstuck

Five Steps to Getting Unstuck	Polarity Intelligent Leaders
1. Understand and respect the values of those who are stuck holding on to current values or ways of thinking and doing	• Treat both Poles as equally important • Lead by being 100% present with the person(s) • Actively listen and are aware of their point of view and their values • Ask questions to gain clarity and understanding • Affirm values by saying, "What I hear you saying is ..."
2. Understand and respect the fears of those holding on to current values	• Check their biases at the door • Actively listen and are aware of the fears that exist around their preferred Pole • Ask questions to gain clarity and understanding • Affirm fears by saying, "What I hear you saying is ..."
3. Ask, "How can we reach what we are going after ..."	• Share the intention to achieve a shared purpose together and to tap everyone's wisdom • See the human capacity in every person • Are role models for every person having a role in gaining "what we are going after" while ...
4. ... without letting go of the values of those holding on ...	• ... reassuring that their values will not be let go of • Communicates with candor and diplomacy • Invites silence and reflection to gain clarity and share wisdom ...
5. ... so that we can move toward a Greater Purpose that works for *both* groups"	• Demonstrates how to establish a shared purpose by moving both groups toward a Greater Purpose

Becoming a polarity intelligent leader is a journey *so* worth taking. It changes the outcomes of your life and the lives of others for a greater good. How do you become such a leader? You embody Polarity Intelligence.

Becoming an Exemplary Leader by Embodying Polarity Intelligence

1. Lead with a Passion for Being Polarity Intelligent

Most leaders are passionate about their purpose and making a difference in the world. There is something you care deeply about, and you want to make an impact.

For us, it started with wanting to improve the healthcare system but has evolved to wanting to improve the way individuals in *all* areas lead. For you, it could be improving the education system, a sector in the business industry, the environment, governmental policies, you name it.

But you also lead in your family and your community, and you're likely constantly looking for areas where you can help make things better. It brings great joy to make a difference. But you know that alone you cannot make that difference. It takes a team, and a great leader is passionate about growing their team into the best they can be, giving team members great recognition along the way.

As a leader moving toward being unconsciously competent in Polarity Intelligence, once you experience the benefits of being polarity intelligent, it's a given that you'll be passionate about seeing others become polarity intelligent as well.

2. Apply the Principles of Polarity Intelligence

If you're learning about Polarity Intelligence for the first time, you're fortunate to have so many resources available to you. We had to learn about the principles and skills bit by bit over several years and by turning to many sources.

Beginning with a limited view, we misdiagnosed polarities as problems, and as you know by now, that means that we kept experiencing the same issues over and over. Only when we recognized the power of integrating a polarity mindset with healthy relationships and meaningful dialogue skills, were we able to see the full view and become unconsciously competent at Polarity Intelligence.

This book is the result of our years of gathering the best resources, and we are grateful we can help you master this critical leadership competency.

Keep the concepts you learned about here top of mind. When you run into a challenge, don't do what we did and what you've likely been doing for decades and jump into problem-solving mode. Instead, pause and ask yourself, "Is this a problem? A polarity? Or could it be *both*?"

Polarity intelligent leaders are fully aware of the top polarities in their field of work. They know how polarities show up and are actively looking for them. So start looking for patterns of recurring issues. Identify what the Poles are that you are experiencing. Uncover the outcomes associated with each Pole and make it visible by mapping it out.

Remember, we have tools available for download at Polarityintelligence. com. You can print these out and use them as worksheets.

3. Start with Personal Polarities

To grow your Polarity Intelligence, start by paying attention to the challenges that show up in your personal life, ones that impact you and your family. As a reminder, the four primary ways polarities show up are as conflict, repetitive problems, resistance, and complaints with solutions. (Refer to Chapter 3 to review these, should you need.)

Once you've created a Polarity Map for a polarity you'd like to manage, identify your preference Pole. This will require some self-reflection on your part. While still growing in your mastery of Polarity Intelligence, use the available tools to assist you in the process. Download and complete the Identifying Polarities Introspection Tool and Worksheet, or simply journal about your reflections.

While you can download a template of the Polarity Map from our website, you can use the back-of-the-napkin approach and draw your own maps. You may want to start with personal polarities, such as Activity and Rest. You can also try your hand at Caring for Self and Caring for Others.

Next, try your hand at exploring some leadership polarities that you're likely experiencing: Planning and Executing, or Individual and Team.

4. Find Your Practice Fields at Home and Work

As you grow in Polarity Intelligence, it's crucial that you're honest. Once you're real with yourself, you'll learn more about yourself. You can even practice having meaningful dialogue with yourself! In the process, you'll find yourself being authentic with others.

At all times, be ready to engage others in conversation about Polarity Intelligence. Practice using the polarity mindset language, as well as the healthy relationships and meaningful dialogue skills. Having meaningful conversations with a colleague or a friend while you learn about Polarity Intelligence is extremely valuable.

Again, use the resource tools available to you at Polarityintelligence.com. Print the tools, and practice both by yourself and with others. Look for practice fields to engage others in the process of strengthening your Polarity Intelligence.

Friends and Family: When friends and family members share with you about a struggle they're having, either at work or in a personal area, be listening for challenges that are polarities. Use your new dialogue skills to learn more. Then, if they wish to hear your thoughts, share that you have a perspective that may help them look at their challenge in a new way.

Create a safe place for yourself to introduce a polarity and engage the friend or family member in the process. Keep it simple by using a blank piece of paper or the back-of-a-napkin approach.

Here are some tips for starting to share about polarities with others:

- Share that their challenge may require a both/and approach
- If they'd like to know more—our experience is that folks usually do want to know more—show them quickly what it entails
  - Draw your map on the back of a napkin or piece of paper
  - Clarify and get consensus on the Poles and Greater Purpose
  - Start with *their* preference Pole, then identify the outcomes
  - Discuss the simultaneous Action Steps to achieve the Positive Outcomes for both Poles
  - Determine what the Early Warning Signs are for when there's too much focus on either of the Poles

Work: As you become comfortable using Polarity Intelligence skills—moving from conscious competence to unconscious competence—it is valuable to practice having the same type of conversations at work.

There are two approaches you can take at work to establish some practice fields.

The first is to listen for the ongoing problems and challenges your team or colleagues face, just like you can do with friends and family. Then you can take them through the same process as above. This works especially well during one-on-ones.

The second approach is to be proactive when you know there is a key polarity that is impacting you and your team. Map out the polarity on your own, then find an opportunity to walk your team through mapping it out together. Use a flipchart or whiteboard and engage everyone in the process.

Keep it light. Don't make a huge deal of walking them through the process. As you engage others in exploring polarities, it can be fun to watch their lightbulbs turn on as they look at challenges in a new way.

This is a great time to be vulnerable and share your preference Pole, as well as your concerns around the Negative Outcomes and the Deeper Fear. Just be sure to also take time to actively listen to their perspective and be aware of how they're responding.

As you communicate with your team how much you care about the Greater Purpose and work with them to achieve it will create a container of trust for mutual listening. This builds trust, which helps create a culture of Polarity Intelligence, which is the next step in becoming a polarity intelligent leader.

5. Create a Polarity Intelligence Culture

Leaders who are adept at using Polarity Intelligence thrive in a culture steeped in Polarity Intelligence. It makes life so much easier when everyone is on the same page and has this same superpower. One of the benefits of being polarity intelligent that we talked about in Chapter 1 is the power of having a *common language and competency*. As a polarity intelligent leader, it is part of your journey to create a Polarity Intelligence culture.

What core polarities can you begin to leverage that would help you live out the core values of your company or your team? Creating a Polarity Intelligence culture requires intentionality, but we can't do everything at once. At MissingLogic, we set aside time during our quarterly review to identify five core polarities to focus on for the upcoming quarter. At times, they stay the same, but we update them as needed.

Currently, we have five core polarities:
- Productivity and Relationships
- Margin and Mission
- Candor and Diplomacy
- Process and Progress
- Individual and Team

These polarities are baked into our culture, and we're committed to being vigilant about monitoring and leveraging them together. When new team members join the company, they are trained and supported to grow in Polarity Intelligence and the monitoring and managing of these five polarities as well. Decisions become easier because there is a wider span of awareness and intention to actions, and we all work with a common language, focused on team priorities, and living out our shared purpose.

Creating a Polarity Intelligence culture also means being committed to living the principles of Polarity Intelligence, even when it means stepping outside your comfort zone. Sometimes you can feel like a lone wolf when you see a polarity and no one else does, but creating a Polarity Intelligence culture helps to change that.

In such a culture, people know it's safe to step forward and share what they know so others can learn while keeping their focus on the Greater Purpose.

One small way you can start creating a Polarity Intelligence culture is by using both/and perspectives. Use those words often and consistently. People get curious and will ask questions, giving you an opportunity to share about Polarity Intelligence.

It will just be a matter of time before you start hearing others use Polarity Intelligence language and they, too, increase their Polarity Intelligence. Fan the flame by celebrating when a team member demonstrates Polarity Intelligence.

Evolving with a Polarity Intelligence Leadership Community

Being in community with other polarity intelligent leaders is transformational. We've talked with others in our Polarity Intelligence community, wondering out loud if they can imagine leading without being polarity intelligent.

We talk about Gwyneth Paltrow's movie *Sliding Doors* in which her life plays out in two distinct ways. One life path is based on her making it through a train's doors in time to catch the train home. The other life path is based on her missing the train because the doors closed a split second before she could get on the train.

"Can you imagine where you would be on your leadership journey if you had missed the train and never learned about Polarity Intelligence?" we ask. The answer is always no.

For all these leaders, Polarity Intelligence has transformed their leadership style and experience. They cannot imagine going back to only having a problem-solving mindset and not having the skills to identify, manage, and transcend biases so they can focus their actions on achieving a Greater Purpose.

Such leadership communities can be internal to organizations as they commit to becoming a polarity intelligent company. Organizations we work with often develop a Polarity Intelligence resource team that become certified in Polarity Intelligence, continue their learning, and share their Polarity Intelligence with others in their environment.

Polarity Intelligence leadership communities can also be external to a company, and joining such a group, leaders can continue to grow their Polarity Intelligence *together* as they stay on the path of being their best selves, both professionally and personally.

Polarity Intelligent Leaders: The Hope for Our Future

This book was written to expose leaders like you to Polarity Intelligence and to give you the knowledge you need to leverage Polarity Intelligence in all the area where you exert leadership.

Now is the time to make Polarity Intelligence a leadership norm. The past few years (2020–2023) have been eye-opening to the challenges that our humanity faces, and the lack of polarity intelligent leaders in our families, work settings, and the world. As such, we wanted to close this book with a message of hope.

We are driven by the vision of what it would be like if every workplace and home integrated and embodied polarity mindsets, healthy relationships, and meaningful dialogue—the three essential components of Polarity Intelligence.

We are motivated by our deep-seated hope for our children and our children's children that the world will have sustainable Positive Outcomes, Dynamic Balance, and mutual understanding.

We believe it would change the world we all live in.

Overview

- There are ways you can increase your Polarity Intelligence so you can become unconsciously competent at applying it—leveraging polarities as effectively as solving problems, naturally engaging others in the process of leveraging polarities, and asking questions no one else is asking.

- As a polarity intelligent leader, you can help yourself and others get unstuck by applying a five-step process to get unstuck from either/or thinking. And you can become an exemplary leader by embodying Polarity Intelligence.

Reflection Questions

1. Which polarities of a VUCA world do you identify with the most?

2. Looking at the four stages of competence—unconscious incompetence, conscious incompetence, conscious competence, and unconscious competence—which stage are you at in learning to be polarity intelligent?

3. What steps will you take to become unconsciously competent at Polarity Intelligence?

Call to Action

- Practice getting unstuck from either/or thinking.
- At home and at work, practice growing in Polarity Intelligence by applying a polarity mindset, healthy relationships, and meaningful dialogue.
- Create a Polarity Intelligence culture by starting or joining a Polarity Intelligence leadership community.
- Join us in changing the world by leading with Polarity Intelligence.

ABOUT THE AUTHORS

Tracy and Michelle met over thirty years ago and have been collaborative colleagues and dynamic coleaders ever since. Together, they cofounded MissingLogic® to bring Polarity Intelligence—the "missing logic" in leadership—to leaders and organizations.

Dr. Tracy Christopherson is a respiratory therapist. She earned a PhD in interprofessional healthcare studies from Rosalind Franklin University of Medicine and Science. Tracy has helped thousands of individuals and leaders apply Polarity Intelligence in their quest to create healthy, healing, collaborative work cultures and environments.

Michelle Troseth is a nurse, a recognized global thought leader, the past president of the National Academies of Practice, and a fellow in the American Academy of Nursing. Michelle has a Master of Science in nursing and studied nurse–physician relationships and nurse satisfaction. She was recognized as a distinguished alumna of Grand Valley State University.

Tracy and Michelle have over sixty years of combined experience in working as consultants and coaches for healthcare organizations across North America. They are master dialogue facilitators, experts in organizational and interprofessional council infrastructures. They hold polarity certification in PACT™—the Polarity Approach to Continuity and Transformation—as PACT™ Foundations & Professional Applications practitioners.

Tracy and Michelle are the creators of the Dynamic Balance Effect Framework™. They use this framework to support leaders in leveraging Polarity Intelligence to create a dynamic balance between their professional and personal lives so they can be TRU leaders—thriving, resilient, and unstoppable.

Tracy and Michelle's company, MissingLogic, has been featured on CNBC for their work with healthcare organizations and for their Healthy Healing Organization (H2O) Framework™. Leaders in healthcare organizations use the H2O Framework to leverage Polarity Intelligence and create healthy, healing work cultures. This allows leaders and employees to perform at their highest level, feel aligned with their purpose, and deliver the highest quality of care.

Tracy and Michelle frequently speak at national and international leadership conferences on the topics of Polarity Intelligence, Work–Life Balance, and Healthy Work Environments. They are co-hosts of a top healthcare leadership podcast, *Healthcare's MissingLogic.*

Tracy resides in Northern Michigan and Michelle in West Michigan. As best friends, they share a love of travel, golf, and playing cards, especially their epic euchre matches with their husbands, Jerry and Kevin.

ACKNOWLEDGMENTS

We'd like to first acknowledge and express our gratitude for each other. Without each other, this book would not be in your hands. We are blessed to have a common vision and shared purpose that is fueled by our opposing but interdependent strengths. We are a walking polarity and consciously leverage those polarities to keep our friendship and business partnership in a constant virtuous cycle. We are blessed beyond measure.

Our Mentors

Thanks to our incredible mentors Bonnie Wesorick and Barry Johnson.

Bonnie has been our constant companion in life and on the journey of writing this book. We so appreciate all her insights, guidance, and support.

Barry has been a treasured gift for introducing us to polarities and for encouraging us at every step as we became polarity intelligent.

Our Writing Team

Thanks to our wonderful editor, Adele Booysen. Adele was the perfect person to coach us through the book writing and editing process. We are grateful for her beautiful and positive spirit while she walked us through every step. Thanks also to Tara Cooper for proofreading our manuscript with fresh eyes and for all her attention to the details.

Thank you to Karen Anderson from Morgan James Publishing. What a joy it has been going from meeting Karen at a cocktail reception in Franklin, TN, and sharing our book idea with her to her being our publisher. We are forever grateful that our paths crossed and her belief in the missing logic we are bringing to leaders everywhere.

Our Cheer Squad

Thanks to our OG Court of Support: Nancy Beale, Kathy De Figueredo, Ann Shepard, Vicky Tiase, Mari Tietze, and Roberta Young. We thank each one for embracing Polarity Intelligence and applying it to their professional and personal lives every day. They have all transformed because of the sacred practice field that was collectively created and the deep friendships that have been formed. You all rock!

Thanks to our dear friend and colleague Dr. Diane Bradley. Diane is the third musketeer, our just-in-time friend with her calls, visits, cards, and gifts, and she is forever loyal to our cause.

Thanks also to all our amazing clients. You are the ones who knew there was another way to see the world and were open to the possibilities when you lead with Polarity Intelligence. The world will be better because of it, and we are forever grateful.

Our MissingLogic Family

Special thanks to our fabulous Integrator (aka Chief of Operations), Karen Rowlader. Karen joined us when this book was first getting under way, and she made it possible to grow MissingLogic while we prioritized getting the book out the door.

Thanks also to our podcast producer, Travis Moore, virtual assistant Daisy "Jane" Coleta, and marketing coordinator Al Damalerio for cheering us on every step of the way.

Our Children

Thanks for always inspiring us to make the world a better place! Shout outs to Tracy's children, Dan and Jenny, Sarah and Pete, and Eric and Lauren, along with her five amazing grandchildren, and to Michelle's children Scott and Lisa, Travis, and Tyler. You all make us beam with joy and pride.

Our #1 Fan

A special thanks to Michelle's mom, Viona Virginia Troseth (aka St. Vi) who has unquestionably earned the title as our #1 Fan. Thanks, Mom, for all your happy hours, dinners, love, and support for us and MissingLogic.

ADDENDUM

Definitions

Polarities

Polarities are interdependent pairs of values, perspectives, or points of view that appear contradictory but need each other over time to achieve a Greater Purpose that neither could achieve alone. These seemingly contradictory viewpoints can also be referred to as Poles.

Polarity Intelligence

Polarity Intelligence is an intuitive ability to recognize polarities and to understand and balance the invisible energy between two Poles. This requires that you transcend personal biases in order to achieve a Greater Purpose.

Polarity Mindset

A Polarity Mindset is the ability to differentiate between a problem and a polarity while understanding and leveraging the principles that govern polarities.

Meaningful Dialogue

Dialogue is a conversation between two or more people where the parties listen and share in a way that leads to deep understanding and shared meaning. Meaningful dialogue begins with setting intentions and creating an environment for psychological safety and exploration. Meaningful dialogue requires listening and awareness, advocacy and inquiry, candor and diplomacy, as well as silence and reflection.

Polarity Intelligence Principles

Polarity Mindset

1. **Knowing the purpose of interdependent values or points of view (polarities)**
   - Both Poles are equally important
   - Alone, neither Pole can reach the Greater Purpose
   - Tension is good and can be leveraged
2. **Recognizing there is always invisible energy flowing between and around the interdependent pair**
   - When the Positive Outcomes of both Poles are achieved, the energy is positive and flows toward the Greater Purpose
   - When you overemphasize one Pole or overfocus on one and neglect the other, you experience Negative Outcomes of the Pole you focused on
3. **Preventing unintended consequences is possible**
   - The negative consequences of overfocusing on one Pole is a loss of the Positive Outcomes of the opposite Pole
   - To avoid the Deeper Fear, you must simultaneously pay attention to both Poles so you can achieve the Positive Outcomes of each
4. **Leveraging polarities creates sustainable desired outcomes**
   - The only way to leverage a polarity is to implement the Action Steps simultaneously
   - The objective of leveraging a polarity is to achieve a state of dynamic balance
   - When focus is heavily weighted on one Pole, you must place enough focus on the oppositive Pole to maintain the Positive Outcomes of that Pole

Healthy Relationships

1. **Being intentional**
   - A conscious choice to be 100% present and connect at the inner-being or soul level of another person
2. **Establishing a shared purpose**
   - The relationship centers around coming together for a common goal
3. **Recognizing equal responsibility**
   - A relationship driven by accepting mutual responsibility in achieving the shared purpose
4. **Realizing human capacity**
   - The potential in oneself and others to continually learn, grow and become
5. **Balancing relationship with self and other**
   - The dynamic balance between self and other(s) to achieve a shared purpose

6. **Being trustworthy**
   - Knowing personal trustworthiness precedes a trusting relationship with one another

Meaningful Dialogue

1. **Setting intention and creating psychological safety**
   - The clarity of your intention and then sharing your intention with others is the first step in creating a safe container for dialogue
   - The willingness to create a safe place, to be clear on what you desire from the heart, and to be influenced making it possible to achieve shared understanding
   - Welcoming the voice of others in an open and authentic way creating an environment that is safe for interpersonal risk-taking
2. **Actively listening and being aware**
   - The willingness to learn by intense listening to self and others, not to analyze, prove, compete, judge, rescue, fix, or blame
   - Suspending assumptions while listening to others
   - Being aware of all verbal and non-verbal communication and emotions
3. **Balancing advocacy and inquiry**
   - The willingness to share non-scripting thinking and what is behind that thinking, with the intention of exposing, not defending it
   - The willingness to ask genuine questions that dig deeper and uncover insights and new learning
   - Being aware of your personal preference toward advocacy and inquiry to help balance the two during conversation
4. **Leveraging candor and diplomacy**
   - The willingness to speak openly and frankly, with honest beliefs or perceptions, *and to* speak with sensitivity toward the recipient(s) of the message
   - Recognizing both are important for meaningful conversation and achieving a shared understanding
5. **Inviting silence and reflection**
   - The willingness to reflect on lessons learned from personal awareness or words unspoken
   - Recognizing the power of both self and group reflection to reveal wisdom and new learning

Polarity Map®

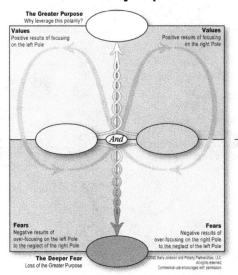

Action Steps
How will you gain or maintain the
positive results from focusing
on the left Pole?
What? Who? By when? Measures?

The Greater Purpose
Why leverage this polarity?

Values
Positive results of focusing
on the left Pole

Values
Positive results of focusing
on the right Pole

Action Steps
How will you gain or maintain the
positive results from focusing
on the right Pole?
What? Who? By when? Measures?

Early Warning Signs
Measurable indicators that will
let you know you are getting into
the downside of the left Pole

And

Early Warning Signs
Measurable indicators that will
let you know you are getting into
the downside of the right Pole

Fears
Negative results of
over-focusing on the left Pole
to the neglect of the right Pole

Fears
Negative results of
over-focusing on the right Pole
to the neglect of the left Pole

The Deeper Fear
Loss of the Greater Purpose

A free ebook edition is available with the purchase of this book.

To claim your free ebook edition:

1. Visit MorganJamesBOGO.com
2. Sign your name CLEARLY in the space
3. Complete the form and submit a photo of the entire copyright page
4. You or your friend can download the ebook to your preferred device

A **FREE** ebook edition is available for you or a friend with the purchase of this print book.

CLEARLY SIGN YOUR NAME ABOVE

Instructions to claim your free ebook edition:
1. Visit MorganJamesBOGO.com
2. Sign your name CLEARLY in the space above
3. Complete the form and submit a photo of this entire page
4. You or your friend can download the ebook to your preferred device

Print & Digital Together Forever.

Snap a photo

Free ebook

Read anywhere

Printed in the USA
CPSIA information can be obtained
at www.ICGtesting.com
JSHW021513220124
55857JS00001B/10